T0156875

A Voice
in the
Village Square

John P. Gawlak Speaks Out
A Compilation of Letters to the Editor
1993 - 2010

iUniverse, Inc.
New York   Bloomington

A Voice in the Village Square
John P. Gawlak Speaks Out

Production Assistance: Carol Gawlak and Charles Gawlak
Cover Art: John Cubeta

iUniverse books may be ordered through booksellers or by contacting:

iUniverse
1663 Liberty Drive
Bloomington, IN 47403
www.iuniverse.com
1-800-Authors (1-800-288-4677)

ISBN: 978-1-4502-2506-9 (sc)
ISBN: 978-1-4502-2652-3 (ebook)

Printed in the United States of America

iUniverse rev. date: 04/23/2010

For the South End Old Timers Athletic Association of Middletown, Connecticut.

A tribute to all my neighbors, friends, classmates, and teammates who were born in the bleakness of the Great Depression, and hardened in the fire of World War II. But, especially for our eleven members who did not return from that war.

Fallen Comrades in World War II
- Stanley Dobrinski
- Joseph Erlick
- Sebatian Faggione
- Edmund Gadzinski
- Julian Gadzinski
- Paul Ribera
- William "Shorty" Roguski
- Louis Ruffino
- Stanley "Socko" Sokolowski
- Anthony "Lanzo" Sledzik
- Frederick Young

Table of Contents

Introduction

I am motivated by a poem I once read. The author eludes me, and it goes thus:

> "Get angry at those
> Who alter your shrines,
> Or the notes of your favorite song."

My father taught me to "speak out" on issues I find unfair and unjust to challenge and engage public officials' injudicious use of elected office and leaders of institutions who violate the trust of their members and constituents. Nothing encourages wrongdoers more than public silence.

I remember him saying, "Two things happen to you when you lay down: you get stepped on, or you get screwed." Here is a collection of my "Speaking Out," a compilation of letters to the editor that have appeared in the Stamford, Connecticut Advocate. I have yet to be stepped on, or the other alternative.

Dante had an answer for all who choose to remain silent, "The hottest places in Hell are reserved for those who strive to maintain their neutrality when faced with a moral crisis."

The Truth in Journalism

"The primary office of a newspaper is the gathering of news. Comment is free, but facts are sacred. Loyalty to the truth must be uncompromising," Editor, New Hampshire Guardian (1926). The old Chicago city news bureau held fast to the adage: "if your mother tells you she loves you, check it out."

A Voice
in the
Village Square

Take a Stand

Let me awaken your anger, stir your emotions and arouse you to action for a good cause – to oppose the arrogance and excesses of the National Endowment of the Arts. First you must read George F. Will on the subject. He wrote: "The arts," laments Rep. Sidney Yates (D-Ill), will be terribly, terribly hurt by the enormous impact of the 5 percent cut in the NEA's $174.6 million budget." What a sycophant.

What is really hurtful here is the rending of the moral fabric of our society. Even with the cut, the NEA budget is $39 million larger than federal funding for prevention of breast and cervical cancer. Women of America, wherefore art thou indignation?

I burn inside at the audacity of the NEA to deem wholesome what is pornography, scatology, and deviant behavior. And I am continually amazed at the urgency of the moral mobilization of this country over issues such as Save the Whales, while only a few bold individuals and groups will rise to protest the insidious flauntings of the NEA.

I believe it is time to bring the NEA in line; to make it conform to the code of decency adhered to by the majority of citizens in this great nation. We are slowly losing some of that greatness, because we have failed to act in the past.

It is time to make our elected officials in Washington know how we feel.

8/15/93

Dear Editor:

About President Clinton: How can you have faith in a man who hides his cigars in a hollowed out Bible? Dan Quayle could not spell potato, and Clinton cannot discern what constitutes sex. I would love to have been a fly on the wall when he was instructing his daughter Chelsea about the birds and the bees.

8/14/98

Americans should not accept Clinton's excuses

To the editor:

Regarding the call to debate the Clinton scandal (Greenwich Time editorial, Sept. 13) I wish to express my opinion.

Let me begin by saying that when lame excuses replace indignation over the president's behavior, we fail as a nation.

It has been proven that the Clinton presidency has been a pattern of lies and deceit, all the way from Gennifer Flowers to Monica Lewinsky, and all the while aided and abetted by Clinton's wife Hillary, and the White House staff of spin meisters.

There are no secrets in Washington, D.C. Everyone in that political sphere knew what was going on, what now has been compiled in Ken Starr's report. Through it all, the silence of the Democrats is proving to be an embarrassment. See them now scurry to save their own political skins. Even U.S. Sen. Joseph Leiberman, D-CT, the new "apostle of morality," turned his courage into cowardice. After his lion-hearted rebuke of Clinton's transgressions, he rendered this rebuke dissolute a few days later.

I recall how this nation, with a wink and a nod, viewed Clinton as a reincarnation of JFK. The women swooned and the men said: "He's our kind of man." Encouraged by this, Clinton took on the bulletproof mantra. To himself, he laughed as we wiped the spittle from our faces when he lied to us on TV. How gallant he was when he told us, "I did not have sexual relations with that woman."

Hillary and her White House spin doctors, with their innocent, shiny faces, bristling with indignation; they told us it was Ken Starr's fault. He was the perpetrator of this evil. Many took the bait and engaged the nonbelievers. Where are their voices now?

The last refuge of scoundrels is confession and contrition. The president can't even do this well, even though his confessions are becoming more solemn as his political execution draws near.

The great tragedy of all this is that the nation ratchets down another notch in our decency, goodness and morality. As a consequence, our youth ratchets up another notch in alcohol and drug abuse, sexual conduct with accompanying teen pregnancy, school violence and disrespect for authority.

In the Navy, we called guys like Clinton "stump jumpers." Some are leaning to give him a second chance. So am I. Let's send him back to Arkansas, so he can practice clearing stumps without stumbling

9/20/98

Good people are sad

To the editor:

This is a story about the pervasive sordidness of modern politics.

Once upon a time in America, two people were on trial: O.J. Simpson for murder and President William Jefferson Clinton for perjury and obstruction of justice. In both cases, the evidence was clear and should have led to conviction. But Johnnie Cochran said Fuhrman did it, the White House shills and the Democratic senators said Starr did it, and a large segment of our population said, "Our pockets are jingling and we don't care who did it."

So a murderer walked; a lying, perjuring, adulterous president walked; and a nation awash in economic euphoria said, "let them all walk." Then O.J. went to the golf course to find out who did it, and the president went back to his Arkansas trailer park to find out who did it and the nation went back to its bank statements and can't be bothered to find out who did it.

All fables should have a happy ending and project a lesson. Well, O.J. is happy, the president is happy and the "let the good times roll" public is happiest of all. The lesson: If the stable of whores rallies around a pimp, you can commit a crime and get away with it. So as these two celebrate their misbegotten victories, the good and decent people silently weep for their children, as they struggle to shield them from this sordidness.

There are many tales about the genie in the bottle and the granting of a wish. My wish would be that we bulldoze Washington, D.C. and move back to Philadelphia; this time, let's get it right.

2/19/99

Babe Ruth support

To the editor:

The recent Senior Babe Ruth World Series was a tribute to classiness and professionalism, not only of baseball interests, but of the supportive community.

Readers should give these people: the Babe Ruth personnel, volunteers, Parks and Recreation workers, sponsors, player hosts, contributors, fans – a pat on the back and some words of appreciation, wherever they run into them. They deserve this.

Special acknowledgement should go to Advocate Sports Editor Bob Kennedy and his sports staff for the excellent coverage in the Advocate of the past history, and the everyday recording of game results and special anecdotes.

All these people make Stamford a great city to live in.

9/1/99

Immoral legacy

To the editor:

Come on! Am I going to be the only one to comment on the State of the Union address?

Once again, President William Jefferson Clinton looked us straight in the eyes, smiled, and like a peacock, spread his plumes and divulged his divine plan of redemption. He will save us all from ourselves. As a savior, his legacy will equal those of former presidents Washington, Lincoln, and FD Roosevelt. The longer he spoke, the more his Democratic colleagues were whipped into a frenzy. They blistered their palms clapping and grew hoarse from repeating "Ain't we got fun."

My reaction was different. To me, Clinton sounded like a boasting town drunk recalling and praising everyone who ever bought him a drink and pledging to pay them back. Have you ever been to the funeral of a town drunk? In low voices, the few people who come whisper of a legacy squandered.

There is a similarity to President Clinton's legacy, for it is of moral turpitude. He cheated our country, he cheated his family, and most of all, he cheated the "man in the glass."

2/14/00

Higher law broken

To the editor:

Bill Clinton and Janet Reno stole our Passover and our Easter when they stole a 6 year old boy at gunpoint. There was a better way, and a better time.

Some see national pride in this ugliness. While they may have upheld the law of the land, they violated a higher law. And their champions applaud this "heroic" action with laudatory intonations of "hooray," when hosanna and hallelujah should have filled that early morn.

The truculence of Reno's raiders to free Elian from his "tomb" cast a long, irreverent shadow on the tomb of the resurrection. The solemness of Good Friday and the joyfulness of Easter Sunday were trampled by a display of federally mandated violence.

You and I – everyday, hardworking, law-abiding citizens – who bear the burden of democracy: How powerless and angry does this make us feel? Readers do not need permission to use their pen, their voice, their vote to express indignation at the indecorous behavior of our public officials. Silence gives consent to the Clintons, the Rambo Renos and all who will come after them.

I equate cheers I hear for them to the cries of that frenzied mob exhorting Pontius Pilate to release Barabbas on the first Good Friday.

5/5/00

Praise for teams

To the editor:

Stamford should be proud of the successes of our high school softball and baseball teams. Coaches Tony Esposito of Stamford High School, Beth Callan of Westhill High School and Tom Kriz of Trinity Catholic and their assorted coaches have provided outstanding leadership to their softball teams.

Tracy Nichols of Trinity Catholic, Bob Augustyn and Frank Scott of Stamford High, Andy DeBrisco of Westhill have provided their baseball teams with the same level of guidance.

This does not happen without strong direction and commitment and support from Athletic Directors Al Gurney and Bruce Cutter, and Principals Tony Pavia, Peter Borchetta and Camille Bingham.

Readers should allow themselves an egotistical twinge and a prideful strutting. Write or call these people. Let them know how you feel. When you see them, give them a pat on the back and some words of appreciation. Have them pass it on to their team members, assistant coaches, support staff, scorekeepers, fans and parents.

Their accomplishments have added to the rich history and heritage of Stamford athletics.

6/20/00

Lighten up America

To the editor:

There is a lot of disappointment, frustration, disgust at the ongoing count, recount, challenge, counter-challenge of the presidential vote. I find it has great possibilities. Here is one: let's give the South another chance at the Civil War. Maybe they will win this time. Then we will elect General Lee as our president, and we will all end up picking cotton for those cotton-picking rebels. Of course, if they lose again, we can always have another recount, and keep giving them chances until they win.

11/16/00

Congratulations to SHS

To the editor:

Congratulations to Coach Mike Smeriglio and his girls' volleyball team at Stamford High School. Coach Smeriglio and his Stamford team follow in the great tradition established by Coach Winnie Hamilton at Westhill and Coach Al Malizia at Trinity Catholic.

All three deserve the respect and admiration of the Stamford community, a community steeped in athletic excellence at all levels of competition.

Let's not forget the high level of sports journalism by the Advocate's sports department, by keeping us informed with quality reporting.

12/3/00

Game is over

To the editor:

Let us look at this past presidential election in a baseball context.

After nine innings, George W. Bush won the game by a close margin. Al Gore was unhappy with the result, and asked the umpires (the Florida Supreme Court) for nine more innings, which they granted. But Bush appealed to the commissioner (US Supreme Court) who ruled that extra innings are not found in the rule book unless the score is tied. Therefore, the game must revert back to the original score and Bush declared the winner.

Fans, being what they are today, erupted in partisan clamor. "Kill the commissioner," said the Gore fans.

I imagine the shouts will go on for some time, but the game is over. Let's lower our voices and accept the result. It belongs in the "hot stove" league now.

12/21/00

Sam Cingari

I was privileged to attend last Monday's State Street Debating Society Testimonial Dinner honoring Sam Cingari as its "Man of the Year." No man in Stamford deserves the honor more than Sam. I want to chide Herb Kohn, Terry Cooke, Leo Gallagher, E. Gaynor Brennan, Don Russell, et al for waiting so long. Despite Sam's business success, charitable endeavors, community involvement, agency service, he deserved the honor on his character alone.

That night, Sam was the standard bearer for all Cingaris, past, present, and future. You equate the whole family with decency, honor, integrity, and grace. These attributes were manifest as Tom Cingari lauded his father with humble eloquence. Tom was a reflection of all Sam's children: Rosemary, John, Michael, David, Tom and Mary.

This nation is looking for those hard elusive answers to all the recent school shootings from Columbine to Santee. "We need gun control," shout the alarmists. No, the answer is not gun control. The answer is the lesson Sam and Cathy Cingari present to us: how a family should be raised and nurtured.

If you have never attended a State Street Debating Society Testimonial Dinner, do yourself a favor and work an invitation. You'll thank me for it

3/20/01

Congratulations, Knights

Congratulations to coaches Bob Augustyn, Frank Scott, Fred Kelley, Glenn Mishuck and the entire Stamford High School baseball team for their CIAC championship season.

Sometimes the best story in sports is when an unheralded team overcomes many obstacles, and in the end, is the last team standing on top of the mountain. That is the story of the 2001 Stamford High School baseball team.

Take a moment to write or call. Tell them you share and appreciate their success. And be proud of our great city, especially the public, parochial and private schools. In spite of the level of success of their sports programs, they produce a healthy blend of athletes and academics.

6/18/01

Twaddle and Prattle

The execution of Timothy McVeigh has unleashed a deluge of capital punishment protestations. Much of it is specious, misdirected concern for the perpetrator, in this case, one without remorse and proud of his diabolism. The State is not a detached enclave of bloodthirsty bureaucrats. The State (we the people), you and me, mandate punishment for crime and the more heinous the crime, the harsher the punishment. We call this Justice; Justice for the victims.

To demand less than McVeigh forfeit his life, would be unjust to the 168 innocent men, women, and children who forfeited their lives to McVeigh's depravity. Count yourself among that 168, because a part of all of us died that day.

Our highest judicial tribunal and scripture offer ample justification for capital punishment. Whenever Jesus spoke, He prefaced His remarks with: "In very truth I tell you…" There is not much truth in what I read in many anti-capital punishment dissertations. In very truth, much of it is twaddle and prattle.

6/25/01

Excusing terror

To the editor:

When the emotions over the World Trade Center horror subsides (if that is ever possible) and the apologists feel safe, be prepared for their literary onslaught. We have seen this before following other national calamities.

The coming apologist apoplexy will inundate us, prefaced by the imprimatur, "I don't condone this, but…." Invariably, the blame of that "but" will fall on us, chronicled by a miasma of past sins.

This deluge of think-tank dissertations will fill our opinion pages and TV talk shows. Be not fooled. They are all a clever subterfuge for condonation, excuse and blame.

The public should be judicious and prepare for the groundswell, but should not be taken in. Apologists, by nature, not only undermine free expression; they do violence to the truth.

On another subject, it is being determined that immigration violations were numerous concerning hijackers. Perhaps it is time to consider a one year moratorium on all immigration until that agency can be bolstered and made foolproof.

9/30/01

Crossed the Line

Three years at sea with the U.S. Navy, I have weathered frightening storms of a sea gone mad. But I am finding it difficult to weather a storm of intellectual madness. There has always been a salient residual of immaturity in many of our college students. This should not be a trait of faculty.

In the shadow of our nation's greatest terrorist carnage, radical faculty and students of CCNY crossed the line with their anti-America pro-terrorist clap-trap. And this is being repeated on many other campuses. Expressions of sympathy for the terrorist and consequent lack of empathy for the victims went too far. This was beyond equivocation, beyond free expression.

As a suffering city and a suffering nation struggle with their grief, it was despicable, deplorable disrespect shown the heroism of our finest and bravest at Ground Zero, and the numbing sorrow of the bereaved victims' families. The enormity of loss: lives, property, security, economic stability is yet to be fathomed. Try as you might, no logical deduction can ascertain any grievance worthy of this kind of redress.

The real cause was fanatical, murderous insane hatred, under the guise of religious fervor. To publicly sympathize with the perpetrators is unregenerate absence of reason. We will deal forcefully, as we must, with the perpetrators. But we must also deal with this radical campus element, who for too long have run amok in their twisted causes.

Free expression is to be respected, but when the form of the expression becomes egregious, it must be questioned and challenged. Campus radicals escape from themselves by hiding behind a self-imposed immunity on their high perch of pedagogy. In this case, they must be called to account. This must not go unanswered. This newspaper could not print my suggestions, as I simmer in clenched-fist outrage. A slap alongside the head would be a fine start.

Gutless and spineless administrators and their governing boards, who have failed to act in the past, must now get some backbone. This is no time for hedge-hopping or queasy gizzards. If they don't, it is time to make our ire and indignation known to the Governors and Legislators who appoint them. It is time to pull the reins, and call a halt to public displays of reckless and unforgivable insensitivity at our colleges and universities.

We owe this to all those who still lie in the rubble in defense of their profaned honor. All who advocate anti-America pro-terrorist sentiment betray the core fabric of our great nation, because they do violence to the sacred memory of the innocent dead and their families.

10/13/01

Bishop's folly

I see the Episcopal bishops have joined the academe in anti-America pro-terrorist leanings. One wears the robe of piety, the other the robe of intellect. Yet, both display an audacious absence of reason. The bishops say we are deserving of the willful, fanatical murderous terrorism because of "affluence." Cardinal Edward Eagan chimes in with "our misdeeds were responsible." To claim the terrorists are vindicated for 3000 murders of innocent people, and willful destruction of incalculable property, because we are free and prosperous is noodled self-righteousness by the clergy and stilted verbiage by the intellectuals. It is a clumsy attempt to gain favor with their God, high-minded insensitivity, and vacuous self-preening. And they wonder why church attendance is declining. For the clergy to accept the tenet that these terrorist attacks are retribution for our failure to invoke the "preferential option of the poor" is to lie, cheat, and steal solace from 3000 grieving families in need of empathy and comfort. Has their piety become arthritic and creaky??? Have they manned soup kitchens so long that morsels become the moral equivalent of murder?? Evil-doing is justified in the quest to slake hunger??? Just how do these bishops equate the increasing anthrax attacks to their starving children??? The demands of discipleship go beyond blame for a hungry world. I now will always be wary of Episcopal bishops bearing signs: "feed the hungry lest the Apocalypse be lost."

10/16/01

Slick Willie still at it

Former President William Jefferson Clinton was paid $100,000 to delude an audience and excuse himself as he addressed 450 business, political, and religious leaders. It was a wooly, fuzzy, self-cleansing diatribe. "Fight poverty to kill terrorism," he said. The 19 hijackers were not aggrieved by poverty or hunger. They were fanatical, murderous terrorists. Schooled in nihilism, they had one aim: kill and destroy all who do not believe as they do. Clinton hugs a lie, is applauded, and is generously paid.

Charles Krauthammer, noted national columnist, in his recent essay, chillingly tells us the real cause of terrorism. It has nothing to do with poverty and hunger. He cites Nobel Prize author V.S. Naipaul from an address to world leaders in Melbourne before the twin towers attack, "We are within reach of great nihilistic forces that have undone civilization." In places like Afghanistan, "religion has been turned by some into a kind of nihilism, where people wish to destroy their past and their culture…to be pure. They are enraged about the world and they wish to pull it down." This kind of fury and fanaticism is unappeasable. It knows no social, economic, or political solution. "You cannot converge with this (position) because it holds that your life is worthless and your beliefs are criminal and should be extirpated."

Our foe does not want our money, our food, our hand in peace. He wants us dead and destroyed, so he can purify himself. This is their Armageddon, and they believe they are the "good guys." This is the real cause of all the recent terrorist attacks we have endured. It wasn't the world poverty to be eliminated. Clinton's idea has merit for the teeming poverty of India, Africa, Central and South America. The crushing poverty of these countries has never been the breeding grounds for the terrorists he speaks of.

Clinton bears some of the burden for the destruction and deaths of those recent attacks. In his two terms in office, it was the consequences of his peccancies that led to decreased vigilance that made it easier for the hijackers to fulfill their suicide missions. In his total immersion to defend himself from scandals of his own making, he took his hands off the wheel, and national security was compromised. Evil needs no reason to wreak havoc, but give Bill Clinton $100,000, and he will come up with one.

11/26/01

Christmas, 2001

With the terrorist attacks of 9/11 in mind, as we gather at our tables on this Christmas Day of 2001, let us be mindful of the victims and their families, especially the children. Let us be mindful of the empty chairs and sadness at their dinner tables. Let us also be mindful, and ask for safekeeping of our servicemen and women overseas. I can relate to that personally. As a young man, I spent three Christmases at sea aboard a U.S. Navy ship. However, I am troubled by one aspect. Some of our spiritual leadership have laid blame on the U.S. What I would rather hear is the scope of anger we should carry, and how to respond to it. Let us gather at our Christmas tables on Christmas Day, but with empathy for the victims and their families. Merry Christmas everyone, God bless us all, and God bless America.

12/14/01

Taking the fifth

The unsavory virtue of pleading the Fifth Amendment, long the exclusive domain of the Mafia, is now being courageously invoked by corporate America. It has become the moral high ground of powerful and privileged top level executives of Enron. The present congressional hearings are reminiscent of the Mafia hearings of the 60's. Remember Joe Valachi, the Mafia whistle blower, who enlightened us to the term Cosa Nostra, the implications of a white carnation being placed in your lapel, and the parade of Mafia hierarchy invoking the fifth?

We all knew this was criminal high-dodgery. The same legal maneuver being used by Enron executives today, has become a dogmatic ukase of self-absolvement.

The Advocate recently featured an article depicting the meaning of flowers and plants. I have gleaned from that list the plants you will find in the garden of these Enron executives: 1. flytrap – deceit; 2. cabbage – profits; 3. hellebore – scandal; 4. almond – perfidy; 5. tall sunflower – haughtiness.

And all the Enron employees who have lost their life savings, I'm sure their gardens are overrun with marigolds which stand for grief.

2/9/02

Church and its believers have been wounded

To the editor:

On Good Friday, a Roman soldier pierced the side of Jesus. Today, a horde of revelations about priestly pedophilia and its audacious cover-up have pierced the side of the faithful. It has become a soul-churning mutilation of the spirit for both the community of believers and the unerring and apostolic priesthood that now flinch under public and parochial scrutiny.

Hartford Courant columnist Denis Horgan writes: "Princes of the church looked away, while soldiers of the church pillaged the innocence of children. The heart aches imagining such an affront."

Recently, a New York bishop said in defense of this church betrayal: "I am a shepherd, not a policeman."

"I will wrestle the devil in defense of our children," would have been a more appropriate response.

Judicial interdiction, not religious indemnification, is needed here. There is a law written across the universe that states: harsh sanctions for harsh criminal offenses against children. The church has no right to abrogate the law.

Just how does one reconcile an aching discipleship with the abject dereliction of certain hierarchy that allowed the continuous violation of children? Jesus foresaw the evil of pedophilia and gave church leaders a stern dictate of how to deal with ignominy. In Matthew 18:1-10, where Jesus delineates the virtue of childhood, he goes on to say: "But were a man to be an occasion to fall to any of these little ones who believe in me, it would be better for him to have a stone from a donkey-mill tied to his neck, and be drowned in the open sea." The late Bishop Fulton J. Sheen wrote: "The greatest betrayers are those who have been cradled in the sacred associations of Christ and His church."

The community of believers in the church – my church - elected shepherds in its origin. Leadership qualities and unequivocal religious standing were the standards of selection. What are today's' standards in our corporate-structured church? Corrosive secrecy brings on criticism.

3/24/02

23

Ivy Faculty Trumps Catholic Hierarchy

In a New Haven courtroom, former Yale professor Antonio Lasaga was sentenced to twenty years for repeatedly raping a little boy, and obsessively collecting tens of thousands of images depicting sexual torture of children. Lady Wisdom and the angels wept in that courtroom at the statements given by three Ivy League professors in defense of their colleague. "He is in his most productive years," said Hubert L. Barnes, "when you penalize Tony for his indiscretion, you penalize society." Princeton trained professor, Hiroshi Ohmoto, said, "I don't believe Tony had any sexual interest in boys. His hands may have slipped when playing with the boy, and the mistake was construed as fondling." Heinrich D. Holland, who taught at Harvard, said, "All of us in science are expendable, but the loss of the most capable is felt the most strongly."

Prosecutor David Strollo was incredulous after hearing these statements, and said, "in all my years as prosecutor, I have never heard people deliver comments so disconnected with reality." The prosecutor read a letter from the victim to the judge. He is so filled with anguish, that he is ready to explode, and implores the judge to punish the perpetrator for what he did to him. We have here a new "ETHOS": elitist intellect of that Ivy League mutual admiration society calls for professional respect for a colleague to trump indignation.

Institutions define themselves by how they respond to the call of justice. These Ivy schools, in their storied pedagogy have remained bereft of human dignity and conscience. How do we grasp this infinite intelligence of Ivy academe that saunters so deep and interminably, so inward and bereft of reality? It is so devastatingly inscrutable; it shakes the rhythm of the cosmos of decency. Do you doubt that the Ivy Hall pedigree hold the treasures of wisdom, the secrets of science, where all knowledge of mankind abide? To me, I see a hidden abyss of spiritual darkness, and unredeemable guilt. Head knowledge is worthless unless accompanied by submission of will and right action.

6/10/02

Skakel conviction

To the editor:

Did defense attorney Michael Sherman overplay Michael Skakel's Kennedy kinship? After Chappaquiddick, Palm Beach, and various sundry offenses, did "we the people" call in the Kennedy "marker?" Did we draw that long overdue line in the sand?

I personally feel what made the difference in Skakel's conviction was a well-prepared, no frills prosecutor besting a showboat defense attorney. It was hard-nose against glitz; a city slicker underestimating the "hick."

Members of this jury were intelligent, perceptive and averse to guile. They rendered a judicious verdict based on a homespun, heart-clutching summation, vs. the defense's razzle-dazzle hijinks.

7/15/02

Another scandal

To the editor:

Just when the horrible sexual abuse scandals of the Catholic Church seem on the wane, another flare goes up, and it is again headline news. Rogue priests keep stepping out of the mist and adding a new chapter. They preach the true gospel on Sunday. On Monday, they write their own lines.

Bishop William Lori, a refreshing change of leadership, acts decisively in removing Father Gerald Devore from his post as pastor of St. Maurice Church (Advocate News, 9/1). The notorious sexual molester, Father Laurence Brett, now a fugitive from justice, is hiding in St. Maarten. Father Devore knew this, but didn't tell.

Illicit secrecy carries its own condemnation. The true calling of priesthood mandates that Father Devore reach out to the children whom Father Brett devastated.

For too long, the parish community was pressed to increase its Sunday collections. This call was constant. I now know why we were going broke. St. Maarten's lifestyle can be expensive.

I admire and respect Bishop Lori. But if he returns Father Devore as pastor to St. Maurice, my parish, he will join two of the biggest scandalizers of the church: Cardinal Bernard Law and Cardinal Edward Egan. I will personally lead a protest and advocate a mass exodus of the parish community.

Throughout all this, I am reminded of the words of Brooks Atkinson, "I have no objection to churches, so long as they do not interfere with God's work."

9/14/02

UConn's Calhoun shows lack of class

Desmond Conner, Hartford Courant sportswriter, captured the essence of Coach Jim Calhoun's disgraceful behavior at the recent University of Connecticut against UMass game. After scoring only 9 points in the first half, the crowd booed the UConn team unmercifully. Conner stated the crowd was out of line, but Coach Calhoun even more so, when he gestured to the crowd to rain down even more boos. And he got them louder and more frenzied.

This was a classless act from a classy coach. I was there, and it shocked and embarrassed me. For a minute, I thought I was watching Bobby Knight. This was sheer humiliation, and that is never acceptable, no matter the forum, or from whom it comes.

Purists will excuse this as a tool of motivation. They say it worked because of the terrific second half comeback. Hidden behind that spirited play were unforgettable wounds induced by humiliation.

All of us, on occasion, are capable of manifesting the dark side of our Sunday, but never in front of our children or grandchildren.

The more I read and see of the lousiness that litters the landscape of sports today at all levels, the more I wonder just who it is that flies over the cuckoo's nest: us or them.

12/22/02

John Walker Lindh begins prison term

To the editor:

I was amused to read in Thursday's (2/20/03) Hartford Courant that John Walker Lindh, now inmate #45426083, will begin serving his twenty year sentence for his service with the Taliban. He will not be doing hard time for the hard crime of treason that he deserves. Instead, he is being sent to one of those "soft" federal country clubs at jobs such as "plumbing, painting, and landscaping." At this "prison," he can also relax in the TV room, and check the Koran out of the library.

At the time, I joined the legion of American veterans who were dismayed at the ludicrous light sentence of John Walker Lindh. I say ludicrous because selling pot near a school brings a tougher sentence. Twenty years for treason, treachery, and betrayal. It amounts to one year for every time he squeezed the trigger and felled an Afghan. And, he gets a free pass for the grenades he threw.

I do wonder about John Walker Lindh. With his AK-47, how many Afghans did he kill? And how many American servicemen and women his tender Taliban heart was determined to kill? The silicone-augmented sylph, Jane Fonda, became the anathema of the Vietnam War. The war on terrorism produced the purulent John Walker Lindh.

We must extract a stern measure of justice from those who perpetrate murderous mayhem under the guise of religious fervor. To do less is to detract from the honored memory of all innocent victims. In this case, a tough-talking president acted with temerity. This mushy moment may come to haunt him in 2004.

2/20/03

Church group isn't subversive

Just when the murmurs of the sexual abuse scandals are abating, another clarion call interrupts the settling residue. Why does my church keep shooting the shingles off the steeple? Bishop William Lori of Bridgeport will not allow the Voice of the Faithful to meet on church property (Connecticut Post. March 30: "Bishop's Stance Angers Activists).

Voice of the Faithful is being treated as a group of subversives: heretic dissidents bent on overthrowing the hierarchy. In reality, they are ardent, loyal, faithful parishioners who have provided financial support and invaluable leadership to the churches in which they are not allowed to meet.

Bishop Lori claims, "The goals of the group are not in keeping with church teachings." That is disingenuous. This evasiveness must be engaged, and the Voice of the Faithful is rising to the challenge. I have lauded the bishop in the past for his strong leadership; but this is a ruling he should rescind.

After the cover up of sexual abuse scandals was exposed, many presiding bishops hid behind spokesman or lawyers. But the burden of shame fell on the faithful and the core of priests who are not malefactors. Having no form of redress to mitigate shame, the Voice of the Faithful organized to seek an equal voice to ensure that such an abuse of authority by church hierarchy doesn't happen again. That is their goal: to work hand in hand with the diocesan leadership to eradicate the stigma and be a partner to corrective measures.

The simplicity of the church as envisioned by Jesus Christ – "Wherever two or more are gathered in my name, I am among them" -is unrecognizable today. The College of Cardinals, the Curia, the Book of Canon Law and the various confraternities at the Vatican are not of Jesus' making. He railed against these structures in the church of his own time.

4/12/03

Gore plus Lieberman equation

When Al Gore chose Joe Lieberman as his candidate for the vice-presidency, it became an equation: T+V=ExO. Translation: when a trollop chooses a virgin to be by his side it becomes expiation by osmosis. And weren't you proud of Gore when he made that dashing pronouncement: "I am my own man?" When did this miracle happen? All Al Gore did these past eight years is follow Clinton around with a pooper scooper.

Our beloved native son, Joe Lieberman is highly respected for his good judgment, but choosing to become a sani-flush for Al Gore is not one of them.

5/35/03

Taxation can ruin YMCA

No one needs to delineate what the YMCA is, whom it serves, or the other profound purposes of its mission. It is a not for profit community serving agency. People are its business, especially needy youth and adults. The YMCA touches the lives of more people in a redeeming fashion than any other social serving agency. Historically, the YMCA has been a beacon and a haven for community service. Membership fees, program rates, and room rentals are based on subsistence scales to keep the organization operational. Nobody makes money or profits from the fee structure.

More than likely, there is a yearly struggle to meet its annual budget. For these reasons, the YMCA has been tax-exempt. It needs no justification for this time-honored privilege. The city of Stamford, citing an obscure court ruling, wants to strip the YMCA of its exemption and place it on the tax rolls. This financial burden will change the face of the YMCA, and will probably lead to its closure. It simply cannot operate as it has in the past if this added taxation were allowed to stand. The good people of Stamford must come to the support of the YMCA. Let the city officials know how harmful this taxation can be. Or, there may be no YMCA to serve the needy of this city as it has done so well for the past 100 years. What then, will the city do to replace it?

6/5/03

Bishops betray the faithful again

It wasn't the poor choice of words, but the steely determination of Frank Keating to fulfill his task of eradicating the Church of sexually predatory Priests and Bishops who cover for them. Appointed by the Bishops themselves to chair the National Review Board, Mr. Keating faced daunting resistance. His commission became unraveled by the secrecy, inapproachability, and self-imposed unaccountability some Bishops ordained for themselves. Failure to cooperate with the review board's quest for information, these recalcitrant Bishops tainted the ones that did comply.

I am puzzled why a successor to the Apostles would stonewall the most diligent effort yet developed to keep children safe and arrest this destructive scandal. Some Bishops confer upon themselves the Divine right of Kings. They invented the Roman Dialogue: I'll do the talking, you listen. A staunch demand for silence and deference, Mr. Keating bristled when faced with this. While he should have measured his words, do not misinterpret their meaning as to the truth. The same failed leadership that caused the Church scandals fails again.

In appointing the National Review Board, The United States Conference of American Bishops offered the injured and shamed faithful, hope. Hope that those who fill the pews on Sunday will be able to revere, respect and trust their Priests and Bishops again. But this latest episode defines an arrogance and self-importance, and discloses a hierarchy that cannot, and will not discipline itself, and again betrays the Church. The Bishops called for reform but refuse to reform themselves, and those who had something to hide deemed Mr. Keating an adversary.

Change must come from the faithful. They must rediscover their voice and demand all tainted in scandal be removed. The Voice of the Faithful and the Voice of the Clergy were responsible for Bishop Law's removal, and can be instrumental for bringing about change, and restoring the Church to prominence as founded by Jesus Christ.

7/7/03

Oh say can you see

Pope John Paul II has fired the first salvo over Fort Sumpter (gay I do's), and in the "rockets red glare," Op-Ed and Point of View pages of our national newspapers will be ablaze with pro's and con's. This will be no civil debate. It will take on a din of "scorched earth" and "take no prisoners." In His own church, the Pope maintains it is acceptable to have a homosexual priesthood as long as they remain chaste. Sorry, Your Holiness, but discovering a chaste homosexual is as rare as finding a white crow. If you wish to learn of the extent of homosexuality in the Catholic Church, especially in the Seminaries, read Good Bye, Good Men by Michael S. Rose.

A number of bishops, who disgracefully allowed a pack of homosexual and pedophile priests to pillage the innocence of children, are responsible for the ongoing sexual scandals in the Church. Add to that the dismal abdication of responsibility by the Pope, and his Curia in Rome, and you have a media frenzy rivaling Clinton/Lewinsky.

Nothing encourages wrongdoers more than silence. The "pray, pay, and obeyers" remained silent when offending priests and bishops were called to account. I predict the vast majority of Americans will remain silent in the upcoming firestorm over homosexual marriages. Dante had an answer for all who choose to remain silent: the hottest places in Hell are reserved for those who strive to maintain their neutrality when faced with a moral crisis.

8/6/03

Where are we headed?

To the editor:

If you have visited the Air Force Academy in Colorado Springs, at the parade grounds, carved into a wall in large letters is the academy honor code: "We will not lie, cheat, or steal, nor tolerate among us anyone who does," Noble aspirations, but ignoble reality.

In the September 8th issue of TIME magazine, you will find these statistics related to female cadets at the academy:

1. 11.7% of female graduates from the class of 2003 were victims of rape or attempted rape.

2. 22.3% of female cadets were pressured for "sexual favors."

3. 68.7% of female cadets had been victims of sexual harassment.

In light of these revelations, the sexual scandals of the Catholic Church, and the corporate corruption scandals of Enron, Arthur Anderson, World Com, Adelphia, and Tyco, isn't it fair to say our country has some major problems? The first is a problem of leadership in our public, corporate, and religious institutions. The second is a much deeper problem in American culture at large, a crisis in personal moral character at the grassroots level.

The Reverend Charles J. Chaput, Archbishop of Denver, in a speech to the Denver Rotary, cites an article from the Denver Post (this letter is dotted with anecdotes from that speech). The article reported that because of the inadequate ethical formation of incoming cadets, the Air Force Academy has established a sort of Morality 101 program to bring the cadets up to speed. According to the statistic of the September 8th TIME magazine, this apparently didn't work. These incoming cadets were the cream of a generation that will run our country in 20 years. And many of them needed a class in ethics?

Now that's a problem for every aspect of our national leadership, and it also points to a deeper problem in American life of personal moral integrity. There is a shortage everywhere of ethical rectitude, especially in high places. It's a flaw that has been growing for decades. Nixon and Watergate, Clinton and Lewinsky, Bush and weapons of mass destruction, are symptoms of the same illness.

Where do we begin to bring about change? It all starts with us as individuals. We all have the same vocation to trumpet personal moral integrity, personal fidelity to people and principles. If each of us leads by example, perhaps trust and respect can be restored to all levels of public leadership.

10/15/03

Genuflect to Celebrity

To the editor:

When the sun comes up, spiders leave their web and seek prey. When the sun goes down, the spiders of the entertainment world would seek out each other to devour a critical public.

The saintly Liz Taylor schmoozes with the fallen Michael Jackson (still dressed for Halloween), and inveighs the accusations of child molestation (again). And the legions of Michael's followers, here and abroad, cry out for the blood of the accuser, a cancer stricken child. Bordering on worship and bereft of reason, they are frenzy driven.

Perverted loyalty makes all subsequent actions paltry. We have seen this before: O.J., the Clintons, P. Diddy. And today we are seeing it in Kobe Bryant. Celebrity is revered, but the accuser is deemed a ghoul.

Hollywood, the Rappers, Rock and Rollers assault us with impunity with their words, their actions, their dress, their lifestyle. They get away with it and grow bolder because the vast majority of good people do nothing.

We can learn from crows. During the change in seasons, a large congregation assembles in the deep forest; raucously berate the transgressor whose behavior endangers the flock, and one by one peck out his feathers. Why are the animals smarter than we are?

11/24/03

Corruption's roots

To the editor:

Political corruption has become endemic in our state – Mayor Giordano of Waterbury, Mayor Ganim of Bridgeport and now Gov. John G. Rowland.

But corruption is not confined to politics. Note the recent rash in corporations, Wall Street, academia, the military and even the Catholic and Anglican churches.

To look for cause and effect, where do we start? Does it begin as political ambition develops? Is it learned as an apprentice? Is it inherited? Or is it determined by personal Armageddons, where evil overcomes our propensity for good?

Adam and Eve succumbed to it. I don't know where or when corruption takes hold, but we all surely know where it culminates.

Ernest Hemingway posed the riddle of the frozen tiger in his novel "The Snows of Kilimanjaro." He challenged us to discern why the tiger left the safe confines of the jungle to meet his end in the foreboding elements above the tree line.

I have not solved that riddle, neither can I demystify the rubrics of personal corruption, but I suppose those who engage in it are like Hemingway's tiger.

1/18/04

Tulip eating deer

To the editor:

During a harsh winter, deer regularly enter my back yard to feed on acorns I leave for the squirrels. Every few years my huge oak tree is endowed with double the normal yield of acorns. The squirrels knock most of them down, and I find it impossible to rake them all up. Now I'm happy to provide these critters with sustenance during difficult winters, but the deer overstay their welcome.

As Spring approaches and the crocuses and snowbelles peek from the snow, I daily check for the first shoots of my tulips and daffodils. I am heartened as they inch upward. After reaching about four inches, they suddenly disappear. All is left is stubble at ground level. The crocuses are nibbled away, also.

At first, I blamed other animals, but on close scrutiny, I find deer tracks in the soft sod.

Now I've had my garden trampled by my grandchildren as a ball goes astray during play. I don't get mad, but I softly admonish them to be more careful. Can anyone tell me how to keep my composure with the deer? Shooting is not an option.

I raise my flowers to give away, but I am being denied an act of generosity. The Gospel is steeped with the need for forgiveness. Can an animal be forgiven?

4/1/04

Voice of the Faithful unduly criticized

To the editor:

Bishop William Lori and his spokesman, Joseph McAleer, are engaged in juvenile bashing of the Voice of the Faithful. In the past, I have lauded the Bishop for his strong leadership and perceptive guidance. But recent statements coming from his office pertaining to the Voice of the Faithful are disturbing to me, and are destroying the good will of many parishioners and the public. Here is what they say: "the goals of the group are not in keeping with church teaching" Hartford Courant, (3/3/03). "Their agenda seeks to reinvent the Catholic Church and diminish the essential teaching and core value of the Catholic Faith" (Stamford Advocate. 4/20/03). Sorry, Bishop, but this is disingenuous and abandonment of some truth. It certainly is not studied and tempered judgment you would expect from a successor of the Apostles. Members of the Voice of the Faithful are as compliant of church teaching as the Bishop himself.

It was some of Lori's fellow Bishops who sinfully and criminally allowed our children to be serially sexually violated. To shift the focus is a ploy. The scandal caused the burden of shame, the Voice of the Faithful organized to seek an equal voice, to ensure this abuse of authority by church hierarchy doesn't happen again. That is their goal: to work hand –in-hand with the Diocesan leadership to eradicate the stigma, and be a partner to corrective measures. The Bishop's insistence not to enter into a conciliatory dialogue with the Voice of the Faithful, will result into a series of ugly exchanges, where nobody wins, and all are left scarred.

The Voice of the Faithful is the flock re-discovering its voice. A voice long stilled by that so-called Roman dialogue: "I'll do the talking, you listen." A stern demand of silence and deference from both clergy and laity, lest the "chain of authority be broken." This type of leadership is reminiscent of "the good ole boys in the back room." What we need are echoes of that first gathering in the Upper Room.

4/3/04

She's back

Politics engenders strange bedfellows. Wasn't that a smoothie with Hilary and John Kerry dreamily beaming into each others' eyes at a rally at City College of New York? She seems to be saying, "Blaze the trail for me, big guy, I want to ride it myself in 2008."

Just when you think the boat of bad memories has left the dock, it springs a leak and the hangover returns. Visions of Lewinsky, impeachment, Whitewater, ill-advised pardons, misplaced FBI files, stolen items from the White House, like sugar plums come dancing by.

I've always been puzzled by the Clinton mystique. Immune to shame, masters of vanity, wizards at compromising the truth, bereft of Cicero's gift of moral wisdom, steeped in self-serving counsel, they have become the darlings of the nation, strange how others romanticize noble savages. C. S. Lewis said that popular culture shaped by the reigning liberals has afflicted many with "chronological snobbery," the attitude that everything modern and current is "ipso facto," superior, enlightened and advanced. To the "chronological snob," the past (moral wisdom of the ages, eternal truths) is archaic and dead, outdated and useless: a form of backwardness and ignorance that the contemporary world has outgrown and transcended. The Clintons and the Kerrys and much of Washington, D.C. are today's "chronological snobs." Can anyone be proud of the political bleakness we face in November?

4/10/04

God created the institution of marriage

To the editor:

The volleys over same sex marriages are increasing in number and intensity. It reminds me of old- time political campaigning. I'll give you an example: in the 1884 Grover Cleveland/James Blaine contest, Cleveland admitted he fathered an illegitimate child. The Blaine forces marched through the streets chanting, "Ma, Ma, where's my Pa?"

The Cleveland contingent would counter with, "Going to the White House, ha, ha, ha."

The same kind of exchanges are being made today as to biblical references. Citing chapter and verse, the "salt of the earth" stand firm, while the original thinkers dribble around the text with whimsical delineations.

I am not making this up. When God made Adam from a clod of earth, he saw the need for companionship, so he took a rib from Adam and fashioned Eve. God blessed them, creating the institution of marriage between man and woman, and commanded them to increase and multiply, fill the earth and subdue it.

Without usurping God's greater wisdom, is there anybody out there who can tell me how this command can be fulfilled by joining two Adams...or two Eves?

4/15/04

Religion and Political Expediency

To the editor:

Machiavelli, in The Prince, made political expediency an eternal truth. He stamped indelibly, "the end justifies the means." Now, let's tie them together.

In the 1928 presidential election, Al Smith was defeated by Herbert Hoover, aided by a barrage of "Romanism," and a "pipeline to the Pope." In 1960, John F. Kennedy won over Richard Nixon dodging these missiles by disavowing his Catholicism in public life. Today, John Kerry, New Jersey Governor Jim McGreevey, and all Catholic office holders, face the cannon fire of their Bishops. Like Mario Cuomo and Geraldine Ferraro before them, they claim personal opposition, but public acclamation to abortion. This is political expediency at its foremost.

Because of this stand, Cuomo and Ferraro faced excommunication by John Cardinal O'Connor. Their Bishops threaten Kerry and McGreevey with denial of communion. A true hypocrite is one who ceases to perceive his or her own deception. They live contrary to their beliefs, and fail to obey the imperative on behalf of truth and life.

This is an unhealthy fracture between public behavior and personal belief. With prudence and a spirit of reasonable comprise, elected officials should inform their actions with their religious and moral beliefs, to act on their principles, even if we do not agree with them. Otherwise, how can you respect and trust them when they personally believe one thing, but publicly do another.

In the recent Democratic primaries, Joe Lieberman hid his Judaism under a basket, and it cost him dearly. The spiritual soundness of President George W. Bush is being severely tested. So far, it seems, he has engaged our country in an unjust war. Weapons of mass destruction have not been found, and proof of Saddam Hussein's involvement in 9/11 is non-existent. Political expediency is not Jacob's ladder, but it can be a slippery slope.

5/3/04

Kerry no Kennedy

To the editor:

Arianna Huffington, in her op-ed article in the May 21 New York Daily News, cites how John Kerry is in a unique position to complete Robert F. Kennedy's unfinished mission of ending a misguided war, returning real compassion to our domestic agenda, and bringing us together as a nation. She makes comparisons between our current war in Iraq and Vietnam. If John Kerry is to fulfill Mr. Kennedy's latent mission, he better change his style. Mr. Kennedy was popular, soft spoken, and in control of his emotions. To win favor, public discourse should be reasoned and measured.

Mr. Kerry's incessant cavil is not an ingratiating quality. Civility is needed here. I am in favor of that old adage, "get angry at those who would alter your shrines or the notes of your favorite songs." But in the process, please do not frighten the children.

6/12/04

Kerry loses screw

Engaging in war is a dangerous and deadly business, no matter what level of education you have attained. Senator John Kerry knows this as he saw this up close during the Vietnam War. But, he blundered when he told a group of students at Pasadena City College that those who apply themselves in study deserve immunity. Slackers end up manning the ramparts in Iraq. If I recall correctly, college students who studied hard and did their homework, conferred upon themselves this immunity by running to Canada during the Vietnam era.

Mr. Kerry epitomizes the synergism of viral partisanship. "Gotcha Politics" so rancid, that tongues fail to unravel they are so knotted in hatred for the opposition. Congressman Charles Rangel is another icon of partisan harmony, calling Vice-President Cheney a "son of a bitch." I may sound intrepid, but given a choice, I would hunt quail with Mr. Cheney than play Scrabble with Messrs. Kerry and Rangel.

Me thinks Senator Kerry, former "swift boat" Captain, has sheared a pin and slipped his propeller ("screw" in Navy lingo), and is adrift. Somebody toss him a paddle. He needs help.

6/25/04

One-eyed squirrel

It is time for a human-interest story. With the passing of the 4th of July, it is time to set aside the political fireworks as well.

I have become fond of a one-eyed squirrel who feeds on the acorns from my oak tree. He has a strange gait. He tilts his head to see from his one good eye, and trundles and stumbles sideways. The other squirrels seem to be aware of his handicap, and do not chase him away.

When the acorns are depleted, I toss out peanuts. He isn't fast enough to get his share, so he waddles to my side, tilts his head to look up at me, and I make sure he is fed. He keeps coming back until he has his fill (usually four or five will do).

Sometimes he waits on the back porch. When he feels I'm too slow in responding he pitter-patters on the storm door with his front paws.

When my wife goes out, and I hear her scream, it is time to hide. She yells at me for traumatizing them both, as she almost steps on him. Because of this, when we shop at the market, I have standing orders: "no peanuts in the shopping cart." Nobody ever said life is easy.

Let me conclude by making a comparison. There is ample evidence that the politicos who populate Hartford and Washington run the affairs of the state and nation like that one-eyed squirrel: stumbling and trundling, and at times, underfoot.

7/6/04 and 1/18/10

Clinton's legacy will always be Monica

Monica Lewinsky was as much a central figure in the autobiography of Bill Clinton's <u>My Life</u>. She received short shrift in the book, but in a recent interview, rises to purport the truth, which she claims Bill Clinton is devoid of.

There are many Biblical references that portend the heaviest of sins lie in the violation of innocence. Monica claims hers was a love story, clandestine, but reciprocated with gallantry. But after the fall, she learns it was her lover's salacious appetite that moved the tryst along.

What is disturbing, even today, is that more people question the veracity of innocence over the leerful reputation of the offender.

Men and women of substance make a contrite admission when they do wrong, and vow to redress the harm.

In all his television interviews, Bill Clinton skirts personal responsibility and shifts blame (right wing conspiracy, Kenneth Starr, vengeful press, etc.).

The legacy of great presidents such as John Adams, Abraham Lincoln, and Harry Truman, has been their strong moral code.

The legacy of Bill Clinton will always be Monica Lewinsky, and 957 pages of <u>My Life</u> will not redeem it.

7/13/04

The saga of "Socks"

Senator John Kerry is striving to ride the coat tails of the Clintons to the White House. "Kerry's party, but Clintons the stars," writes Cindy Adams in the New York Post. But President Bush can guarantee his reelection if he capitalizes on a Clinton gaffe, mysteriously absent in his autobiography, My Life.

The loveable Clinton cat, "Socks," was the darling of the nation in the early Clinton years. "Socks" was discarded when the Clintons left the White House, but was fortunate to find a home with his long time secretary. Cat lovers (and they are legion) know the cruelty when a life-long pet is exiled.

To fill the void, Clinton acquired a dog called "Buddy." Darwin implied, "it is a violation of natural law to transfer affinity from one species to another." Clinton thoughtlessly left the door open; "Buddy" got loose, and was run over by an automobile.

New York Judge Edwin Torres, upset about the increasing apathy of the public, said, "a society that loses its sense of outrage is doomed to extinction."

I believe if President Bush can muster the outrage of cat and dog lovers in this nation, to keep the sad and tear-inducing stories of "Socks" and "Buddy" ever present, he will avoid the fate of his father: a one term President.

7/25/04

All candidates alike

To the editor:

I wish to respond to "Voters need to recognize the unpleasant truth" (Advocate Letters from Readers, July 30).

John Kerry stated at the Democratic convention, "I will start by telling the truth to the American people." He better start because he hasn't told us much truth this past year. Politicians rarely tell the truth. They attain high office because they're proficient at "spin and weave." How they dance around it!

The letter-writer implores us to open our eyes and vote for a positive future. Sorry, but our last opportunity for that was when George Washington was elected. Washington began to see the birth of political parties during his second term and, because of partisan politics, began to have difficulty with the Senate, especially when establishing treaties. Two years after his retirement, he was asked to "stand once again for the presidency." Party politics had taken over the country by then, and he said, "The parties can now set up a broomstick and get it elected."

James Monroe, beleaguered by the partisan bickering, said, "I have always considered the existence of political parties the curse of the nation."

The wretchedness we have seen in our presidents (especially, recently) has been the spawn of the two party system. The tears of joy brought to the eyes of the letter writer while watching the Democratic convention by "the thought of having intelligent thinking people in the White House" were folly. There are no thinking people in either party "who look at the real issues for Americans" when they gain the White House. Their only issues are self serving.

The power and the wealth of the party in office run the country. The sitting president better abide by its command if he or she wishes to enjoy the ride.

I would advise the letter-writer not to wish so fervently for change. No matter which party gets in, it becomes more of the same. The faces change, but the trickery goes on. And "we the people" will continue writing letters to our newspaper, complaining about abuses of power.

8/10/04

Democrats wasted "our" money

If I were to categorize the recent Democratic convention in Boston, it must be deemed a hate-filled, anger-fest of "Bush bashing," followed by a litany of promises of how they can run the country "better." There way of "doing it better" is a call to socialism: a nationalization of resources with the unspoken cost that will require exorbitant tax hikes.

After the razzle-dazzle of Bill Clinton, it was an unending march to the podium of sleep inducers. Expecting a high level, thought-provoking political dialogue, we were given a cure for insomnia.

Here are some highlights: for Al Gore and Ted Kennedy, it was a call to end "class warfare." Al Sharpton said, "The black vote is not for sale." Has he ever appeared in public not selling something? After Jimmy Carter's momentous Camp David peace accord between Menachim Begin and Anwar Sadat, he should have gone to his admirable venue of Habitat for Humanity. Just what did Madeline Albright say? Why wasn't anyone paying attention to Joe Lieberman? General Clark thought he was addressing the troops at Fort Hood. "Corn Pone" Edwards will oversee our conversion to social equity. And why even mention Ron Reagan, Jr.?

Let us not forget the dignified and lady-like responses from the feminine side, from Theresa Heinz Kerry's "shove it" to Hilary's "You go girl." We have heard from Whoopi Goldberg and Linda Ronstadt. What can we expect from Barbra Streisand and Denise Rich? To listen to the craven rants of Pelosi and Feinstein, the line between the genders blurs.

Compared to Bob Dole and George H.W. Bush, John Kerry's war record is back page. Dole and the senior Bush never talked about their war experiences publicly, and never used them for political advantage.

I shall sum up the Democratic convention as 4 days of twaddle and prattle, and I will give you some real political insight. Without Monica, there would be no 957 pages of "My Life." Hilary would be at home keeping a light on for Chelsea had Rudy Giuliano not contracted prostate cancer during the senatorial race. Also, I am not looking forward to the Republican Convention; it will also be a sham and a disgraceful waste of an awful lot of money.

8/12/04

A grain of wheat

To the editor:

It was unchrist-like of a Bishop to divest a little girl of her sacramental union with Jesus Christ, because of the ingredients of a wafer; a mark of a church in decline that needs some serious self-examination. One need not be a spiritual giant to realize the wisdom of Solomon is not needed to rectify this. We have all been reading about that little girl in New Jersey whose Bishop invalidated her First Communion. A province reserved for God alone. Vatican authority, steeped in Canon Law, dictates the Communion wafer must be made of wheat to replicate the bread Jesus shared with his apostles at the Last Supper. This little girl (Haley Waldman, age 8) has a rare digestive disorder (Celiac-Sprue Disease), a genetic intolerance for gluten (a food protein contained in wheat). People such as Haley have an allergic reaction when they consume it, sometimes, fatal. Her Mother asked her Pastor to substitute a gluten-free wafer for her First Communion. Bound by church dogma, he refused, hence the controversy.

Jesus was very resilient in all his occasions of healing. Calling on that same resiliency, a saintly Priest (and there are many) volunteered to offer a gluten-free wafer. He acted in the truth of his calling, in a spirit-filled fulfillment, to insure that an innocent sick child be allowed "to come and be touched by Jesus," through the sacrament of her First Communion. His judgment was that the Spirit of Jesus must prevail over Canon Law; that Vatican authority must never supersede the authority of Christ. He uses the Gospel of Mark 10:13-16 for justification.

After a hard day in the vineyard, Jesus went off alone to rest and to pray. Mothers were bringing their children for him to touch. Thinking Jesus did not want to be disturbed his Disciples scolded those who were doing so. Seeing this, Jesus became indignant, and said to his Disciples, "Let the children come to me. Don't hinder them, for of such is the kingdom of God." He embraced and blessed them, laying his hands on them.

Jesus makes no mention as to composition of bread as a requirement to enter His Father's kingdom. In this case, whom do you say acted more in the childlike spirit demanded by Jesus: this special Priest, or all the Bishops of Rome?

9/12/04

Republican Convention

Since I critiqued the Democratic Convention, it is only fair I do likewise for the recent Republican gathering. But, first I want to say the 2004 Presidential election has turned into "two cats on the back fence howling at each other." The constant bickering and denunciations convey a lack of shared purpose (make sure 9/11 never happens again). We are facing one of our greatest threats since WWII, and this compelling and defining issue is what needs to be central. What we have instead is a catfight between Kerry's Vietnam medals and George W. Bush's National Guard Service. But, back to the Convention: Rudy Giuliani prepped for his 2008 run; Arnold Schwartzenager needs to be reminded his Terminator role is fiction; John McCain needs to improve his laconic style for his forceful message to be more effective; Zell Miller was harsh and "raw meat"; Dick Cheney was "Johnny-one-note"; the Bush twins could have displayed some maturity; the Republican women (Laura Bush, Elizabeth Dole) were a refreshing change of warmth, grace and charm as opposed to the hostile and pugnacious Democratic fairer sex; George W. Bush was a preening President presiding over a rollicking Texas barbecue replete with snide remarks about Kerry's Swift Boat heroics.

Political foresight: if you think this election has turned into "take no prisoners," wait until Rudy takes on Hilary in 2008. It is a pleasure to see Chelsea Clinton overcome her dysfunctional family and become such a gracious and elegant young lady.

9/16/04

Pass the pepto

To the editor:

Now that the swift Boat Captain (John Kerry) and his squishy tongued wife have run aground, let an old Navy man tell you, that when you enter uncharted waters, you'd better know the channel markers.

While I have reservations about the reelected president, he was the necessary choice of a bad tandem. If Bush and Kerry are the best this great nation has to offer for our highest office, then we'd better revisit how political leadership is developed.

We now read how the starting gun is raised for the 2008 election. Must we again endure those stomach-turning political ads that injure our intelligence? Hilary to the front for the Democrats; Giuliani and McCain Republican top dogs.

Please pass the Pepto Bismol.

11/12/04

Election Analysis

I am trying to decipher what is being heralded by the political "experts" as the great "moral virtues" victory of George W. Bush. All the analysis proclaims a majority of Americans are fed up with the amoral lifestyle attributed to the Democrats. Pandering to Hollywood and entertainment types comes to mind. Where else are public profanity, pornography, adulation of adultery, and sodomite symmetry exalted? I find this to be psycho-pap and the reading of signs. The truth is John Kerry had no clear message. I snidefully proclaim his wife had a better one.

Bush gave Kerry an invitation to defeat him (no weapons of mass destruction; tax cuts for the wealthy; record deficits; a wavering economy with consequent job loss). But Kerry chose to make war on the war, and the war defeated him.

But the learned analyzers of political history chose to hold a séance, and the voices from above drifted down to "morality gone astray." There is some truth to that, and if President Bush uses some of his "political capital" for amelioration, then I will buy into his "moral victory." And this for the Democrats in 2008: there will be no victory if Michael Moore, Bill Clinton, Dan Rather, Bruce Springsteen, and Barbra Streisand are called on for endorsement.

12/3/04

Red nosed Rudy gets rummaged

The Grinches are at it again. The Board of Education of Maplewood, New Jersey has ruled that Christmas Carols are forbidden to be sung in schools, including "Rudolph the Red Nosed Reindeer." Separation of church and state has crept into children's fairy tales.

There has been a steady erosion of reference to God in many facets of our culture. An attempt was recently made to eliminate God from our coins and the pledge of allegiance. But courage prevailed over timidity.

Our founding fathers looked to God for counsel and guidance, and wrote Him into our pledges, proclamations, declarations and preambles. The Grinches have been chipping away at this bedrock. It is time for believers to do some chipping of our own.

President George W. Bush was reelected by a mandate to return to "moral values." I am surprised that only 61 million of us voted him "political capital" to counter the nonsense of the Grinches.

12/10/04

Vote of approval

I am writing to concur with Carolyn L. Huber in her letter to the Editor (Views of Freedom, 12/2/04). She refers to the essence of many Americans being abused by the Far Left and the Liberals in this country taking away the belief in all absolute. How refreshing to see someone engage the culture changers. She lauds the 61 million voters who voted against morality gone astray.

There has been a steady erosion of reference to God in our public discourse. Our founding fathers looked to God for guidance and counsel, and wrote Him into our pledges, proclamations, declarations, and pronouncements. But the culture changers have been chipping away at the bedrock.

This last election showed that the majority of Americans are fed up with the moral pollution stemming from the entertainment industry, and the corruption of corporate executives and elected officials. The public abhors hearing profanity, pornography, adulation of adultery, and freelance abortion. Abortion signals the real moral depth of society. The justification of killing innocent life destroyed by whimsy of choice; one of Satan's greatest seductions is that one can never do evil so that good may come of it.

President George W. Bush was reelected by a mandate to return to judicious morality. 61 million of us voted him "political capital" to counter the culture changers and balance the spiritual equation.

12/11/04

Weak commissioner fails baseball

George Steinbrenner, adding the "Big Unit" to his baseball juggernaut is tantamount to Alexander the Great adding another division to his world conquering army. What is most surprising is the weasly and wimpy response of Commissioner "Bud" Selig. Is there a Viagra he can take to overcome his impotence?

Former Commissioners Bowie Kuhn and Bart Giammati would have vetoed this trade for the good of baseball. Kennesaw "Mountain" Landis would have grabbed Steinbrenner by the ear and led him to the woodshed.

Don't concede the pennant to the Yankees yet. A-Rod failed to bring it home last year. The Red Sox were not " lucky." Napoleon met his Waterloo and Goliath fell to David. Wouldn't it be a charm if "Mighty Casey" strikes out again?

1/7/05

Height of insensitivity

The Courant needs to revisit the protocol that qualifies the elements for "Front Page" news. The defeat of the UConn women's basketball team by Tennessee in a regular season game does not. And, the half-page photo of a tearful Ann Strother was shameless insensitivity. It was an obscene display of bad taste. In your enthusiasm for embarrassment, are you seeking a "ratings bonanza"? The whole state that saw that game was in sympathy with that young lady. Why did you choose humiliation? You have been in business long enough to know the standards for decency in journalism. I hope you apply them in the future. Leave the clever digs to Jacobs on the sports page.

1/9/05

Doom and gloom changed to glory

To the editor:

Several weeks ago, UConn faithful were calling for the scalp of women's basketball coach Geno Auriemma. Still seeking the right combination to put on the floor, Auriemma held fast as he sought the right pieces to the puzzle. After four untimely losses, many fans abandoned hope for the glory days of Taurasi, Bird, Svet, and Lobo.

After a victory against Tennessee slipped from his grasp, Auriemma knew he had found the key to turn his team from doom to gloom to the road to the Promised Land. He had the key, but like the parable of the lost coin, it takes diligence and faith to overcome the agony of the search.

Just how do you burnish raw talent you know is destined for greatness, especially when the people who fill the arena (like those who filled the Coliseum to scream for the blood of the Gladiators) demand you win today, not tomorrow? Do you know how close Geno was to thumbs down by his faithful? Nobody is immune from doubt. And a hostile media makes that malignancy grow, and batter you to submission.

We all underestimate the beacon that led our state university's legions to the mountaintop of women's basketball. And when the light flickered a few times, we said "uh-oh!" Have heart. The wave is back. Is it possible that someone greater than Taurasi (whose name was chiseled into the rafters at Gampel) is in our midst? If you saw Charde Houston play against Texas (I know it's only a sneak preview) can you imagine what that raw ingot will look like as a finished product? Move over, Diana. Company is coming.

When the Apostles faltered once, Jesus admonished thusly: "Oh, You of little faith!" Like John the Baptist, I am calling upon the UConn faithful to repent of your queasy and weasly unfaithfulness to Geno Auriemma now that he has you back cheering instead of grumbling.

1/23/05

The Rather syndrome

Dan Rather and his four "Bunco" sources recently fired by CBS, could have benefited from the wisdom of the following: "The primary office of a newspaper is the gathering of news. Comment is free, but facts are sacred. Loyalty to truth must be uncompromising." Editor Manchester NH, Guardian (1926). The old Chicago City News Bureau held fast to the adage: "if your mother tells you she loves you, check it out."

What was demoralizing was watching Mr. Rather defend himself and his sources; the skillful turn of a phrase; clever sleight of hand; slippery language. The usual hackneyed talking points that become the all-encompassing yardstick where right and wrong are lost.

The Clintons were notorious in its use. And, it seems contagious as President Bush seems afflicted. What is most puzzling to me is that this lack of rectitude escapes public incrimination. Bush was re-elected president, and the Clintons gain popularity and adoration. Malfeasance of our public officials must be engaged. Martin Luther King said, "our lives begin to end the day we become silent about things that matter."

1/30/05

Justice demands execution of Michael Ross

To the editor:

The mind twisting on-again, off-again execution of serial killer Michael Ross has turned into a legal volleyball game: point for the prosecution; side out for the defense; back and forth; endless legal wrangling where there is no more room on the scoreboard to tally the results. Just when is overtime too long? We already are going on 20+ years.

The death penalty is the proper punishment deemed for Michael Ross for the heinous crimes he committed (rape and strangulation of eight young girls); the penalty favored by "we the people" and written into the law of the state. Why is there no mention of the unspeakable horror of these young girls or the soul-searing grief of their families?

All I read is the need to spare the life of a criminal who forfeited his right to live. This judicial shell game is an affront to the victims and their families and due justice denied.

Rights of criminals are the spawn of the Earl Warren Supreme Court. Law enforcement authorities became criminals each time they made an arrest without permission of the perpetrator. We are seeing the residue of that insanity.

In a poll conducted by Quinnipiac University, 59% of us favor capital punishment. But I'm afraid the opposition will be the winners; not because we will succumb to sheer exhaustion watching the legal mud-wrestling of the never-ending chapters of the Michael Ross saga. It makes you wish for the fulfillment of the famous Shakespearean quote about lawyers.

2/10/05

Judge plays gunslinger

To the editor:

The recent unjudicatory actions of Federal Judge Robert Chatigny in the Michael Ross case abrogated the rule of law the judge has sworn to uphold.

He acted as a gunslinger when he threatened Ross' defense attorney with disbarment. All this was designed to foster his self-serving end to deter Capital Punishment.

In doing so, the judge trampled the will of the majority and his responsibility as an officer of the court.

His two prior postponements of Ross' execution were overturned by a higher court and upheld by the U.S. Supreme Court.

Michael Ross neither wants nor deserves these legal contrivances to save his life, which he forfeited by his heinous crimes. The stale formula of this endless legal wrangling profanes the suffering of the victims (eight young girls raped and strangled), the soul searing grief of the families and fill me with an anger that shivers in my blood.

If you feel the same, do not expire in your lonely silence, call for the removal of this errant judge. For when you compromise yourself to spare the evil of Michael Ross, you dance with the devil.

2/25/05

Reason for execution

To the editor:

Sister Eileen Reilly says Michael Ross' execution was "state-sponsored murder," and beseeches us "do not kill in my name" in her Viewpoint piece (The Advocate, May 18).

Ross' execution was a case of just cause, mandated by "We the People" for unspeakable crimes against eight young girls. Sister Reilly, like Sister Helen Prejean, takes up their cause with a philosophical abstraction that lacks substance.

What is held wrong by an individual has no merit when held right by the preponderant will of society. This is sacred in our democracy.

Sister Reilly was part of a vigil outside the prison during execution. She questions the method of execution (lethal injection) and surmises, "Is there really a decent way to kill someone?"

This is a question she should have asked Ross.

Srs. Reilly and Prejean could win me over to their side – not because they are right, but by using these saner rallying points: the obscene cost to the state for executions, the interminable legal wrangling, the shift of focus from the victims to perpetrators by the media and the unwanted emotional burden imposed on the victims' families.

5/25/05

Justice not served with Sister's book

Sister Helen Prejean, an ardent anti-capital punishment advocate, gained considerable notoriety with her book, <u>Dead Man Walking</u>, recently made into an acclaimed movie.

She is about to release another book on the same subject, titled <u>The Death of Innocents</u>. In the book, she claims judicial flaws and geographical bias (mostly in the South) determine how the death penalty is imposed, especially for minorities.

The good sister writes, "Patterns of implementing the death penalty clearly show that who is killed, and who is spared, is determined largely by local culture – 'our way of doing things' – not by law."

This is a tortured interpretation that needs to be refuted. She sounds like a human daw pecking at the truth, an obfuscation that should be avoided when God is your boss.

I struggle with the mission of the good Sister. She comes down from the mountain bearing the Gospel message that incarnate evil is worthy of redemption. But redemption requires repentance, which is absent in her advocates.

This saps my spiritual energy. Justice would be better served if she used her ruler as much as her prayers, irrespective of the death penalty argument.

6/5/05

Pollution is not our main problem

To the editor:

Without much fanfare, the world press carried news confirming proof of global warming. Debate went back and forth between pro and con scientists, secure in their knowledge that this is really happening. Look for abatement of the shrinking polar ice cap to become our foremost agenda. After all, nobody wants the oceans to creep into our living rooms. Environmental pollution already occupies much of the country's effort.

Try building a doghouse in your back yard without multiple permits from local, state, and federal environmental offices.

While stemming environmental pollution is a noble enterprise, I see a greater danger in the moral pollution of our young in the violent, misogynistic and profanity laced lyrics of rappers, increasingly bold and unfettered nudity, and sexual depictions on screen and in print; school violence; and rampant pornography.

Rap is becoming the basic language of expression for our young people. It seems out of the gutter emotes today's values. If you swim in a sewer with your mouth open, you become like the contents.

The moral spiral of dehumanization of our young needs equal attention as the diminishing polar cap. The late John Cardinal O'Connor of New York City called this the "slide into the moral midnight."

His was the rare courage to engage the permutations of honest and cherished behavior: the kind that profanes the primacy of civility. We should follow his example, as the poet says, "Get angry at those who would alter your shrines or the notes of your favorite song."

7/8/05

Politics and our courts

Today's news carries a running commentary on the daily spats of our two political parties over the appointment of a number of federal judges. They are engaged in a child-like tantrum of name calling that is about to progress into spitting. The decibels rise to the degree of their perceived offense to their sensibilities. With the upcoming hearings to replace Supreme Court Justice Sandra Day O'Connor, this child play is soon to erupt into a preview of Armageddon. Sen. Ted Kennedy is sharpening his sword, and can't wait to play the Samurai. And if Chief Justice William Renquist also retires, as is expected, he'll be strapping on the explosives. Presidents Washington and Monroe foresaw this trend and considered political parties the "curse of the nation."

Since we are talking about our courts, for nearly 200 years tampering with the Establishment Clause (separation of church and state) would run counter to the American historical experience and be seen as self-destructive. Religion was publicly declared, and shaped our government and society.

Patrick M. Garry, a visiting professor at the University of South Dakota Law School, writing in the New Oxford Review, states that beginning in the 1960's and 70's, litigation of frivolous religious issues (school prayer, graduation invocation prayer, etc.) brought a conflict between the Establishment Clause and the Free Exercise Clause (Congress shall not make any laws infringing on the "free exercise" of religion). Most religious litigation since then, says Professor Garry, should have been tried under the Exercise Clause. He states, "Religious liberty is the first freedom protected in the Bill of Rights, followed by free speech." Yet, religion mentioned in public venues can be restricted in ways raw, violent rap lyrics cannot be. Michael Jackson can grab his crotch on national television, and be cheered. You grab your prayer book, and get fined. He cites many other examples: a teacher cannot display a Bible on his desk, but can show condoms and nudity; singing of Christmas Carols is forbidden, but profanity-laced anti-war slogans are allowed; you cannot wear a cross as jewelry in school, but you can display a crucifix immersed in urine as art.

The courts have become cultural supervisors in the realm of tolerance for diverging and opposing attitudes and "lifestyles" (feminism, sexual revolution, "gay" rights) to the exclusion of religious rights. Professor Garry writes: "the aim of most litigation has been the promotion of a religious free America, causing religious discrimination as the only type of discrimination now permitted by current constitutional doctrines."

The framers must be meeting in conclave, boiling in rage, at the abrogation of the cherished document where the truth must never change. The culture changers aim to fill the void with moral relativism, which is spiritual zero.

7/11/05

Latest politics

To the editor:

Political war drums along the Potomac are beginning to rise in crescendo in preparation for the coming 2008 Presidential election. President Bush is in a lame duck term. The Iraqi War is losing public support; his social security overhaul in shambles; and his judicial appointments have become a shooting gallery. From the Democratic camp comes the din of "Fe-Fi-Fo-Fum." Climbing the beanstalk is Hillary Rodham Clinton.

The nation seems to be enamored with this rising star. Her name and face appear daily on our screens and in our newspapers. She hasn't accomplished much as a lawmaker, and even less as a voice of New York. Her photo-ops far exceed the demands of history. But the rhyme and meter of her qualifications to lead this nation in these uncertain and threatening times are shallow, and flawed by the lack of rectitude.

She faces a greater obstacle: her husband, former President William Jefferson Clinton. His persona demands he be "front and center." His viscera will not allow him to be upstaged when it comes to front page. There is a law tattooed on his forehead: "Me first."

Hillary was very accommodating to become invisible during the Lewinsky scandal. Bill is incapable of stepping into the shadows. The biggest news of the election will not be the results but how compromising he will be. And even bigger news will be: what do we call him if Hillary wins? First what? I would suggest "First Stud."

8/25/05

What's going on at UConn

Criminal behavior by some football and basketball players and poor judgment by the administration are becoming embarrassments to our flagship university that should not be winked at as they have in the past.

Loans of cars to coaches and athletic directors for basketball tickets: five football players arrested for firing a pellet gun from a car; two basketball players arrested for stealing laptop computers; and the president is called to account for shoddy construction of student dorms due to lack of proper inspections.

These are the kind of incidents you would expect from Miami, Nebraska, Colorado, or Florida State. Is the University of Connecticut losing institutional control? Who is on watch? Who is at the wheel?

As an old Navy man, when we were underway, we stood watch in the gun tubs four hours on, four hours off. Heaven help you if you fell asleep. It meant Brig time and the possibility of a firing squad. I believe there has been a lot of sleeping on watch at UConn. There is an old military saying: "when you lose a war, you fire the General."

If these incidents continue, we should consider firing the "General" who runs our university, and some of his "Captains" who run the athletic department. Lou Holtz was fired by Notre Dame for trying to lower the academic standards for his football players. Is Coach Jim Calhoun embarking on the same venue?

It is hinted that A.J. Price and Marcus Williams will avoid jail time. Lacking blue steel backbones, history shows this translates to eventual playing time.

To socially redeem wayward youth is laudable. But you become suspect when they are needed to vie for a national championship.

Coach does a cute little dance away from the real problem but he compromises the integrity of the university and sullies the reputation of our great state.

Coach Calhoun says of his arrested players: "These are good kids who did something stupid and selfish. I will not abandon them."

No, Coach, this is criminal activity, not a childish prank. More than a "time out" is needed here.

He is beginning to sound more like a priest but he has a better future as a probation officer.

8/28/05

Supreme Court

Let's put the sniping over the inept response to Hurricane Katrina (local, state, and federal officials all deserve blame) aside for a moment, and comment on the ongoing hearings for chief justice of the Supreme Court. Early press reports indicated nominee John Roberts would be "Borked" by the Democratic "Goon Squad" (Kennedy, Schumer, Biden, Feinstein, et al). I'm puzzled by the muted shrill of Hillary who relishes throwing kidney punches. I see the deft hand of Karl Rove in devising the clever "rope-a-dope" played so skillfully by John Roberts during the hearing. You could read his lips behind his smile: "never laid a glove on me."

Let's not chuckle over our teacups as round two is coming up: Bush's nominee to replace Sandra Day O'Connor. There are demands he nominate a woman, preferably Hispanic, to complete our country's cultural mix. But my preference would be a Native American woman. Long neglected inclusion of the people who were here first, and we shoved aside. This will balance the cultural equation. I long for the mellifluous names they carry (Rising Moon, Eyes Like Stars, Happy Smiles). It would help subside the ongoing rancor over the Indian designations of college and professional athletic teams (Fighting Sioux, Redskins, Seminole Warriors, etc.). We need a respite from the partisan bickering over Katrina, and the truculence of the Supreme Court hearings. We all deserve a needed rest, as there is work to do. Quiet time is becoming harder to abide.

9/16/05

Katrina rhetoric

In the aftermath of Hurricane Katrina, there has been as much political debris (much of it, partisan) as there was in the actual devastation.

President Bush has been singled out as the principal malefactor. But local and state officials deserve equal skewering. When the rhetoric lacks credibility, it becomes intellectually dishonest, and the volume from the Democratic side of the aisle defies common sense.

Large-scale human misery from this natural disaster requires wise and gentle words and reasoned and measured assurances that everyone will help. Fruitful labor is the demand of the moment. But the smothering of human suffering with partisan political platitudes is both vain and vengeful. Crisis and challenge need helping hands that are cooperative.

The time-honored desire of men and women seeking political office is prudent lawmaking to serve society and to transcribe the will of the people who elected them. There has been an erosion of that calling.

Being a lawmaker should be a privilege and an awesome responsibility. Many do justice to this honor. Others misinterpret the shadows around them and concern themselves with combating perceived demons. The principal qualification for political office seems to be an uncanny resilience to deflect scandal.

The fallout from New Orleans proves that James Monroe was right: "Political parties are the scourge of the nation."

10/16/05

Big oil steals Congressional hearing

To the editor:

It was difficult to tell who convened the congressional hearing on big oil obscene profits. It seemed the big oil executives asked the hard questions, and it was the congressional committee members who flinched. The purpose of the hearing was to determine if surtax should be applied to the stunning amount of profits the oil companies amassed by the offensive increase in gas prices.

The oil executives blamed the damage incurred to offshore oil rigs by Hurricane Katrina that caused a gas shortage, necessitating the vulgar gas price increase, that lead to excessive profits.

If I was a committee member, I certainly would have asked why, after four hurricanes ravaged Florida last year, and caused an equal amount of damage to the oilrigs in the Gulf, yet there was no rise in the price of gasoline at the pump?

It is an established fact that President Bush and Vice-President Cheney have heavy investments in big oil companies. Is there a connection?

11/30/05

Horn's hook 'em

To the editor:

The cowboys came to La-La Land (plastic surgeon's paradise) and were told to leave their boots and ten gallon hats outside. Don't spill beer on the rugs, watch out for candles, and keep off the grass. It was a hard command for prairie people. So they knocked the Trojan off his horse, threw their surfboards in a heap, and watched Annie Oakley shoulder the sultry slick-town beach beauties with their thong bikinis and silicon augmented lips and boobs. Hard to find a natural breast in this town.

When it was over, Coach Pete Carroll went back to John Wooden to once again ask, "How is it done?" And a coach with a hick name, Mack Brown, from a hick town, hoisted the trophy. He just stole a game, stole a national championship, stole the headline, but most of all stole history.

With guns blazing, Wyatt Earp (Vince Young) cleaned up Dodge City, and sent the outlaws (Leinart, Bush, White) to Boot Hill. High Noon out duels Hollywood Boulevard.

And now, President Bush will lay down his chain saw, and host a bunch of saddle-sore ranch hands who play football for his beloved university, with a Texas barbecue that will go on forever.

As a side note, sports writers all over the country reach for Nexium to soothe their indigestion from swallowing their computers. You see, they violated their own time-honored writers' code: there is no sure thing in sports.

Also, pass the Nexium to the USC football team. Humble pie sits heavy.

1/6/06

Lieberman is correct

To the editor:

You may not like him, but you can't help but admire his courage to stand tall among political "scolds" who champion partisan causes in high pitch. People forget how close Senator Joe Lieberman was to becoming vice-president, even though an Al Gore presidency would have been more disastrous to our country than the present quagmire of Bush's Iraqi venture. Sen. Lieberman stood bold before, being the only Democrat to publicly denounce Clinton's scandalous Lewinsky sexcapade.

His present stance in support of Bush's war in Iraq is drawing fire from a Democratic insurgency, and a hostile press. History tells us truth-seekers of the past have been stoned, flayed and their heads served on a platter. The din arising from our nation's capital tells me that the practice remains. In that citadel where the truth is tangled and honor is elusive, there isn't enough oil in the world to keep the lamp of Diogenes glowing in his search for the truth, unless he stops by Lieberman's office.

The Senator from Connecticut is right. It is too soon to epithet the war in Vietnam's gloom. Wait for the results before we surrender. And, it is too soon to call for his head. Who knows? He may bump Hillary for his party's top spot in the 2008 elections, if his stance on the war proves prophetic, and he gains popular support. We forget that he pulled the greatest upset in Connecticut political history by defeating Lowell Weicker (considered unbeatable) with his ingenious campaign slogan: "Does a bear sleep in the woods?"

1/6/06

The taking of hostages

To the editor:

The timidity of the British in dealing with Iran over their hostages had me wondering if it would last as long as the 444 days of our own hostage fiasco during Jimmy Carter's presidency. The quavering responses cast a shadow on Britain's redoubtable military history that gave rise to the bold proclamation, "There will always be an England." President Carter futilely engaged Iran in dialogue for over a year. He found prolonged dialogue equates to political impotence.

What was needed by President Carter and British Prime Minister Tony Blair, was the ultimatum, "Get out of Dodge by sundown," especially when both had the resources to enforce it. The Israelis showed how to deal with hostage situations at Entebbe. Prolonged dialogue would have gotten them all killed.

Today's daunting challenges show how desperately we need someone with command and courage. In your opinion, who among our multitude of presidential candidates fits that role? In this increasingly dangerous world, which one is steely enough to lead America into the 21st century? Who do you see possess the mettle to light the watch fires if there is a repeat of the malignant darkness that bled across our skies on 9/11?

No matter your station, you get devoured in this world if you show weakness. People who argue with themselves are like those who disagree with a certain moment in history. I get the feeling that if Britain or any other member of the European Union were subjected to their own 9/11 moment, they would still be waiting for an apology from Osama Bin Laden.

1/20/06

Days of retreat

To the editor:

Ronald Reagan, in his January 25, 1988 Address to Congress, said, "We have left behind the days of retreat." In a recent press release, Hillary Rodham Clinton stated, "If I am elected president, I will end the war." Meaning, she will lead the retreat from Iraq.

There have been too many retreats in our recent history. (Korea, Vietnam, Somalia).) Peace is not the by-product of retreat but defeat. Retreats have worsened situations we set out to remedy. Former presidents Jimmy Carter and Bill Clinton also sanctioned retreat when faced with crises.

World War II and the Cold War had us on the brink of catastrophe. But we had leadership equal to the task. I do not see their equivalent capable of managing today's growing menaces at home and abroad. That includes Hillary. I do not say this with malice or lack of chivalry, but as a sensible and practical appraisal of her resume.

There is nothing in her term as Senator that sets her apart. She has been unproductive and has not authored meaningful legislation. She has not tasted the hard edges of leadership required for crisis management on a world stage. In truth, she is at basement level of statesmanship compared to Golda Meier, Margaret Thatcher, and Indira Ghandi.

In my opinion, she is neither qualified nor worthy of the office of presidency. For the sake of history, for the sake of future generations, we need a president (man or woman) who can command in the crucible of the moment. Let's not cheat ourselves again by heeding her call for retreat.

2/10/06

Get ready for 2008

It is discomforting to see the mess the sitting Republican administration has gotten us into. But, it is equally delusionary to hear how the Democrats will make everything come up roses. Does the shrill vehemence of Kennedy, Biden, Schumer, Pelosi, Feinstein and Boxer indicate a better future for our country? Especially the anger and twisted pronunciations of Hillary the scolding McCaw. Weary grows the public at this dishonorable behavior.

Differ with me if you will, but historical inter-party intransigence has toppled verity and trampled the will of the people. Politics has become the sanctuary of wealth, power and the connected. Governance, as visualized by the founding fathers, has become the new "gold strike." And the fortunes of the 49'ers are the select elite rushing to Washington D.C. to mine their fortunes. Poaching is allowed by those who stake the biggest claim. Lesser ones can only snipe. This is not new, but getting worse. George Washington and James Monroe long ago decried the bane of political parties. The paradigm of both parties has become "the truth lies just over the next hill."

Prepare yourself for 2008 campaign rhetoric: "we will unite the country", "we will restore your confidence in our leadership", "we will cut the fat and reduce our national debt", and "the people have spoken" (the people being Cindy Sheehan and the New York Times). By this logic, we should all be excited by these "Great Expectations."

Arthur Schlesinger wrote, "The truth is, what comes out of Washington, regardless of the party in power, is not a cure, but a dodge." Absent, evasive and distorted. Vote your party in and watch the miscreants get bolder.

The honorable call to political service – to make the right decisions for the common good – has been vaporized by inter-party fratricide. Therefore, I would like to express myself more profanely at the perversion of our governance. But let's just settle for "good golly, Miss Polly."

The truth is that very little truth comes out of the political realm of Washington D.C. The gospel of anti-violence was born here, yet more violence to the truth is committed here than anywhere else. This is where we need to change.

2/18/06

Are we ready for Hillary?

Hillary Rodham Clinton announces her candidacy for president with this bold statement, "As a Senator I will do everything in my power to limit the damage George W. Bush can do." One of seven tasks of Hercules was to bring home the girdle of an Amazon queen. It seems Hillary's is the scalp of President Bush. Harsh words for someone so ladylike. But we should not be surprised as we are seeing women in governance matching the pit-bull tenacity of the men. The "scratch and claw" performances of Pelosi and Boxer are outdoing their male counterparts.

What is lost in this political conversation is the fact that Hillary voted for the damage Bush is inflicting. Now that the war is unraveling, she wants her vote back. Nice bit of Monday morning quarterbacking. Just how do you put the bullet back into the gun after you've pulled the trigger? And she better be careful what she says about the war, because if she wins, the war will be hers.

Maybe I'm being too hard on Hillary. Maybe we need a woman as president. Maybe we should take a chance on her. This country was built by taking chances. And, oh! How we need a feel good story. Maybe she'll get lucky. Maybe she can avoid the trap (that killed the swift boat captain) where a hard question is asked and her scripts and monitors are not available and she fumbles it away.

We have been going through years of apprentice presidencies. (Carter, Clinton, Bush). It is depressing knowing we face another chapter. We are in the midst of some of the most dire and dangerous times of our history. Our need is leadership of courage and substance. Hillary has not been tested. She has not tasted the hard edges of worldwide statesmanship. What we have seen from her is principle sacrificed for ambition, the constant need for popular approval. She is hardened in partisan hegemony, but we have seen no echoes of crisis management on a world stage. If this is the best Washington has to offer, shame on us.

3/9/06

Lost opportunity

In a recent press release, Secretary of State Condoleeza Rice stated, "Yes, I think a black person can be elected president." She does not accept the challenge, and announces she will not run.

This is regrettable news for our country; a country aching for "good" news, because a run-off between Rice and Hillary Clinton would be a "Fight of the century." I can't think of a more exciting match. The possibilities are endless. Foremost is the "burr in the underwear" of the politically correct ensemble, in their cry that national leadership should reflect the mix of our population. They are a loveable crowd, but loud and persistent, like an itch that's hard to reach.

A woman and a black have never been elected to our nation's highest office. This was an opportunity to fulfill one, and possibly both of these omissions. Just picture the magnitude of that engagement.

Jack Kavanaugh, a local author, just published a biography of Gene Tunney, which featured another "fight of the century": Tunney's victory over Jack Dempsey before the largest crowd to ever witness a heavyweight championship bout (100,000), which featured the famous "long count." With Rice's withdrawal we are being denied the feminine equivalent. Sometimes we get cheated out of history's greatest moments.

3/12/06

UConn basketball – missed opportunities

Cut me some slack as I comment on the missed opportunities of the men's and women's UConn basketball teams. Too much has been written about the men's lost chances. Nobody realizes it more than Coach Calhoun, who will carry a knot in his stomach for quite awhile.

As for the women, as flawed as they looked, they had an equal chance to go all the way. Had Barbara Turner had a little help inside, they would have gone to Boston for the Final Four. That help should have come from Charde Houston, whose sporadic play is a mystery. After displaying tremendous potential in her freshman year, she came up with a case of the "yips." I think she became timid, afraid to make a mistake, by the verbal bombardment and screaming meemies of Coach Auriemma. I am not shooting from the lip. You acquire some wisdom after 80 years in the trenches.

Differ with me if you will, but you want to know something? A softer tune might have produced a better result. The lost chances will be lamented and debated long into next season. And if next season produces the same results, perhaps changes should be considered.

Tell me if I'm nuts, but roll this scenario around in your head. Charde transfers to Tennessee, and carves her initials in the rafters when she returns to the Hartford Civic Center. Call me if I'm right.

3/31/06

Hillary challenger

To the Editor:

It is time for a warm, pleasant smile-inducing story on today's political scene.

Kathleen McFarland, a Reagan-era Pentagon spokeswoman, has announced her entry into the Republican Senate primary to take on Sen. Hillary Clinton of New York. Her secret weapon? Niceness.

"I am not an attack person. Partisan politics that are driving us apart need to end."

It's political heresy, but what a welcome change. Oh, how we need to open the window and let in the fresh spring air.

Ms. McFarland is a relative unknown, with poor campaign financing compared to Hillary ($430,000 versus $17 million), but she has a political pedigree. She was protégé of Henry Kissinger and speech writer for former Secretary of Defense Caspar Weinberger.

When asked how she plans to challenge her formidable foe, she quoted George Washington during the dark days of Valley Forge: "It's not up to me; it's up to the creator. But I can wage a campaign that deserves to win."

"What George Washington said is good enough for me," said Ms. McFarland, "it's up to the creator…and the voters.'

I believe the creator is smiling and perhaps toying with the idea of performing the miracles she needs to win.

4/11/06

Bush needs rallying cry

E. Thomas McClanahan's Op-ed article (5/10) "Rhetorical Flaws will Diminish Bush's Legacy," cited the lack of Bush's ability to respond to his critics and rally the country with stirring, forceful, and profound pronouncements. This flaw, says McClanahan, has helped the Democrats, who now have control of Congress, to take command of the war and dictate its conduct.

Bush's finest moment was when he rallied the country after 9/11. Standing atop a heap of debris of the Twin Towers, he announced, "Osama Bin Laden will hear from all of us soon." There has been an absence of a clarion call since.

Former presidents in similar situations have left their mark on history by calling on the country to stand firm and united. Here are some of their epic callings: Lincoln: "a nation divided cannot stand"; John F. Kennedy: "Ask not what your country can do for you, but what you can do for your country"; Reagan: "Mr. Gorbachev, take down this wall," all rallying cries that united the country to a singular mission.

Bush is standing in the rubble of Iraq, and the debris of an intransigent Democratic majority, but he can't find the words to light the campfires of unity. Partisan rigidity has declared the war lost. This is reckless and dangerous. No one really knows what the outcome will be. Bush still has time to bring his "A" game and salvage a positive result.

After Bush cleaned up Afghanistan, he told Saddam Hussein to, "Get out of Dodge by sundown." The Democrats are now the gunslingers, telling him to "Get out of Bagdad." I believe this is premature and ill-advised. They are only "greasing the skids" for themselves, because the war will be theirs if they win in 2008 and the specter of a nuclear Iran on the horizon.

5/12/06

Bishop mishandles scandal

The real scandal emerging, from the scandal, at St. John's Church in Noroton is the subsequent actions of Bishop William Lori. The real culprit, Father Jude Fay, who stole parish funds to finance his homosexual trysts, is becoming invisible. The amount uncovered is placed at $200,000 and counting, and I wonder if the real amount, predicted to be much higher, will ever be revealed.

Father Michael Madden and Bookkeeper Bethany Derario, who exposed the erring father, are replacing him as greater transgressors for being "disobedient" and interfering with the Bishop's investigation. Disobedience now trumps homosexual romps and felony theft. This frumpy charge is a famous response of "bishop-speak" in line with Roman dialogue, "I'll talk, you listen."

Father Madden and Mrs. Derario acted with courage and resolve, and should be lauded, not reprimanded. I will venture to say had other parish priests acted with such "disobedience" much of the sexual abuse scandals could have been averted, or at least greatly diminished. I believe the Bishop is in a snit because he wanted a quiet resolution without media exposure, but the revelations forced his hand. Now his reactions are begetting greater exposure.

It is being suggested this "disobedience" may lead to the termination of Mrs. Derrario, and Father Madden being shipped to Siberia. Sensing this injustice, many parishioners are scathingly voicing their displeasure. Perhaps the Bishop doesn't realize that by shooting the messenger, he shoots himself in the foot.

Stanley Crouch, syndicated columnist of the New York Daily News, is right when he says, "the greatest wounds to the Catholic Church are not the slurs of Hollywood through <u>The DaVinci Code</u> or Madonna, but the ones that are self-inflicted.

5/26/06

Feast or famine

Any call for the reduction of obesity in our children and adults is both urgent to the times and paramount to the need of better health management today. The recent passing of John Kenneth Galbraith reminds me of what he wrote in his novel, The Affluent Society, (1958), "more die in the United States of too much food than of too little."

I was a young lad growing up during the Great Depression, which was a time of "too little." Because of the economic hardships of that time, there wasn't enough food for anyone to become obese. The homeless shelters and soup kitchens of today are minor league compared to the great depression of my time. The whole country was one big bread line and soup kitchen.

Albert Maltz defines the conditions of that time best in his book, New Masses (1932). He describes the protagonist walking the streets of New York, looking for work and a meal: "She was sitting on the stoop. When I walked by, she crossed her legs showing her thighs and winked. I walked over to her. "How about it, Hon?" I said, "Christ, Kid, if I had any dough, I'd rather eat."

Those of us who have been in the trenches for 80 or more years can relate to both these extremes: 1930's (too little), and 1990's (too much). If it's all right with you, I'll choose the hefty side, thank you.

7/25/06

Harvard football: paladins no more

New York Daily News "Sport's Wire" is a daily report of achievements and abasements of athletes in all sports everywhere. We all read it. They are short, factual summations of good and bad sports behavior and results. Reports of booze, sex, drugs, thefts, assaults, and DUI from some of our most notorious universities (University of Miami, Colorado, Nebraska) have become "Ho-Hum." Who can forget the laptop scandal of our own university? Sunday's edition carried a report of Matthew Thomas, captain of Harvard's football team, breaking into his former girl friend's dorm room and assaulting her. Wow!!!

Scandal in Ivy League athletics is as rare as finding a white crow. The Ivy League is respected for their Olympian ideal in competition. Pristine, scholarly, courtly, whose only prize is a laurel wreath. Well, they are paladins no more. When you lose your halo, you come down to the hard-hats. We have seen them all fall: high politics, academe, corporate executors, financial big-wigs, church hierarchy, media moguls. Just where do we go to see and hear about someone who did it clean, did it right? For Carm Cozza, the venerable dean of Ivy League coaches, this must equate to the betrayal of Judas. Homer's <u>Ibid</u> explains it better, "it steals the mind even of the wise."

7/26/06

Bishop to blame for priest's resignation

I occasionally attend the Sunday 5:00 P.M. Mass at St. John's Church in Noroton. The scandal just won't go away (to the Bishop's chagrin), so I went last Sunday to see how the parishioners were reacting to their sudden unwanted prominence. Attendance was less than other Sundays I had attended, and I was surprised to see Father Madden presiding. He seemed more solemn than I remember.

After Mass, the presiding priest greets the congregation on the way out the front door. When it was my turn, I told Father Madden I was a visitor but I wanted to shake the hand of a "real" priest. He got flustered, and had difficulty responding.

Little did I know how deeply the Bishop's forced apology and the vexing spin of his spokesman, Joseph AcAleer, mutilated his spirit and crushed his vocation in a display of raw ecclesiastical power. The Bishop punished the innocent (he "worsened" the investigation), and let the criminal flutter free (an act of compassion) to a secret setting.

This quirky justice is baffling. He makes an innocent priest apologize and sends him on a sabbatical of penance and prayer, but sets a thieving priest free to enjoy the fruits of his crime. I am trying to find some redemption here. Perhaps Father Madden and Mrs. Derrario should consider themselves lucky the church has outlawed burning at the stake.

Bishops are at their best in their insatiable cry for money. And at their worst in dealing with their parish priests: especially Father Madden and Mrs. Derrario, both now gone. And the Bishop hides when he throws the new pastor (Father McGrath) to the wolves at a recent parish meeting to explain it all.

Jesus summons us all to "act justly." The Bishop does violence to that call in his injudicious handling of the troubling scandal at St. John's Church in Noroton. From the outset, had the Bishop used prudence instead of guile, he never would have lost favorable press, a revered priest, and bookkeeper, the good will of one of his key parishes, but most of all, the luster from his halo.

9/2/06

Anti-Semitism factor

To the Editor:

There is a lack of honesty in the sudden and overwhelming bashing of Sen. Joe Lieberman by individuals in the Letter from Readers section and opinion pages.

Just a few years ago, Lieberman was so revered by his own party as to be chosen to run as our vice president. Is it really his support of the Iraq war and the "kiss of death" by President Bush?

I think not. Other prominent Democrats (Hillary Clinton, John Kerry, Chris Dodd) voted for the war, yet have avoided the vilification being heaped upon Lieberman. By surreptitiously withdrawing from the maelstrom, they cloak themselves in immunity.

I will jump into the fire with both feet and proclaim much of the incoming barrages to be veiled and latent anti-Semitism.

9/8/06

Demeaning Politics

To the Editor:

To engage in Political conversations today, you need to be "combat ready." Gone is reason, logic and perspective, guidelines for discussion in a more mannered time of the past.

The past of my time: of real neighborhoods, stay-at-home moms, innocence of movies, and life without Little League. A time when Sunday was truly "a day of rest," lifted the soul and provided a sense of transcendence. Morality was never ambiguous and truth was not relative.

Today's political ads on Television verge on madness. Honorable, respected, learned men and women ravage each other in stupefying baseness. It is savage bloodletting, rife with twisted and distorted facts that make one queasy.

I need someone to answer the questions: "How do winners reclaim their honor and dignity?" "How many showers will regain their respectability?" For you and me: impossible. For a professional politician: not much. Please hurry up and get the elections over with, or am I going to get arrested for doing violence to my television set.

Is there a secret prize, beyond "public service" that drives men and women of high principle to engage in demeaning behavior on a national scale?

11/03/06

Pyrrhic Victory

After the Democrats finish celebrating their enormous election victories, they better start looking over their shoulders.

This assumed "thumping" of President Bush comes with markers. When the cheering stops and they un-wrap the prize they have won, it will turn out to be the same war they convulsed over, although now, the war is theirs to wrestle with.

There is an age-old saying: "Be careful what you ask for." What magic do the Democrats have to secure victory? Generals Grant, Pershing, Eisenhower and MacArhur are not available. I think President Bush pulled a rabbit out of the sand and tossed it into the laps of his most vehement critics. If they've never played hot potato, they better learn in a hurry.

Let's hope they do a better job than the Republicans, because results will determine the 2008 Presidential election. Bad management will leave them like Lady Bird Johnson, who said, "The coach has turned into a pumpkin, and the mice have all run away," as her husband yielded the presidency to Richard Nixon on January 20, 1969.

11/26/06

Why does Knight get a free pass?

Coach Bob Knight massages the jaw of one of his Texas Tech players and gets a free pass from three highly visible ESPN basketball analysts. Dick Vitale, Digger Phelps, and Jay Bilas deflect criticism from the coach as a conspiracy of detractors.

What should have been rebuked comes out sounding like praise. What was clearly shown on national TV screens was physical assault, an act of violence that fits his reputation. This is not an honest defense of a likeable miscreant. It is being disguised as rationale, but it is really "pimping."

Violence has become so prevalent in athletics that it has filtered down to the Pee-Wee (6 year olds) level. Here are nationally respected voices whose advocacy should be used to stem this growing problem, but they add to it.

Leadership demands self-discipline and respect: qualities lacking in Coach Knight's conduct. His volatile behavior on the basketball court is recidivistic, borders on criminal, and breeches the bond of civility. The atmosphere of a Knight-coached game is noted for the quote: "Keep the fire extinguisher handy."

I have often wondered what magical exemption has been conferred on Coach Knight that enables him to rise from the ashes of self-destruction. I'll tell you why. It is because of a gutless array of ESPN announcers; a gutless succession of college administrators; a gutless public who remain silent; a gutless sports media (both print and TV) who fail to condemn his out of control audacity.

Coach Knight's violent outbreaks on and off the basketball court, are so long-standing they defy explanation. Nor should they be excused. But he keeps popping up like bird droppings on your newly washed car.

Reclamation projects are noble, if successful. But success in this case is elusive. There always seems to be a refuge for a scoundrel like Coach Knight. One is always waiting for him at ESPN where he can tell us how he did it "his way" when it should have been the highway.

12/03/06

Political satire

For the moment let's brush aside the blitz of hot air and political snarling, and engage in a light moment. Rare to find in today's "Rumble for the Bundle."

With the onset of diversity, inclusion, tolerance, and political correctness, it is time to overcome the snail-pace assemblage of political evolution. The hue and cry is the need to rectify the omission of certain segments of our population to the office of presidency. Stifle your desire to "vent your spleen," as this is meant to bring a smile, not bile.

We have never elected a woman, a black, or a gay to that lofty office. Hillary and Obama fulfill only one of those requirements, Condoleeza, two. To touch all the bases let me propose the following: we elect a black lesbian, we are home free. Then we can concentrate on electing a Pole, Italian, Hispanic, Irishman, Oriental, etc. We clean that up, we move onto the next category: Catholic, Protestant, Mormon, Hindu, Judaic, Atheist, etc. Get the picture?

12/27/06

Girls should remain as altar servers

There is a lot of "sound and fury" over the recent publicity about girls being replaced as altar servers. Some churches are urging only boys serve on the altar as an inducement to vocations. I say there is room for both.

In the Gospel of Matthew 19:13-15, Jesus rebukes his disciples for trying to prevent the children from coming to Him. He said, "Let the children be, and do not hinder them from coming to me, for as such is the kingdom of Heaven." Note: he does not say, "boys only." He wants the girls, too, not only in the garden, but also on the altar.

I applaud the VOTF (Voice of the Faithful) for castigating those churches that deny girls from serving on the altar of Christ. And I chastise the writer (Advocate, 3/5) for calling VOTF the "Voice of the Dissenters" for doing so.

When the VOTF organized (in response to the sexual abuse scandals) their desire was to work hand in hand with Diocesan officials, in partnership (laity and hierarchy) in solving problems. But Bishop William Lori refused their offer saying, "The goals of the group are not in keeping with church teaching." This is the same kind of Pharasaic accusations often used to put Jesus to the test. I admire the VOTF for speaking out against wrong doing in the church and proposing to work jointly in seeking solutions.

It was the disassembling of the traditions, customs, and practices of the founding church by the second Vatican Council, and the soul-wrenching exposure of the cover-up by many bishops of the priestly sexual abuse scandals that caused the dwindling numbers of the priesthood. The U.S. Conference of American Catholic Bishops has been Frisbee-tossing these problems for decades without resolution. These are the real problems of the church. Chasing little girls off the altar and maligning the VOTF are not the answer.

3/7/07

Notes on our next president

The war grinds on in Iraq, and we all groan under the increasing casualties, both civilian and our military. It is easy to become fatalistic under these circumstances, and grumble about the loss of command. I've always held that the verdict is not in, but I find it harder and harder to hold on to that belief.

The reason we are there (weapons of mass destruction) has proven untenable and I find myself asking, "Is the wheelhouse unmanned?" Am I wrong in stating that this war has been poorly planned, managed and conducted, which, leads to the subject of leadership? Our successful wars have been led by generals, giants in strategy, tactics, and resolve (Washington, Grant, Pershing, Eisenhower, Mac Arthur). Can you name a general of note in this war?

Let's look at the leadership vying to write the next chapter of our nation's history (Hillary, Obama, Edwards, Dodd, McCain, Giuliani and others). Not many have been seasoned for the hard command in crisis management. I give the nod to Giuliani for his handling of the aftermath of 9/11. But I find it difficult to wrap my mind around their partisan rigidity, a militancy to party, not to country.

Mario Cuomo, analyzing the presidential campaign said, "It will be about charisma, money, and lots of bull----. Vision, substance and specifics will be hard to find." This reinforces the growing public perception of their dislike and distrust of politics and politicians. It is early for desperation but listen to some gems: Hillary turning into Harriet Tubman; Obama's dissertation on violence; McCain's hip-hop version of "Bomb, Bomb, Iran;" Edwards's $400 haircut. They are becoming victims of their own poor judgment and fodder for the press.

We have paid dearly for the ineptitude of a bad run of recent presidents. Some, because of their timidity, led us down that dusty road into that gulley of indecisiveness, where you lose control of the outcome and diminish your legacy.

David Halberstram, responding to what he felt was the one central question about Vietnam said, "How so many smart people could have been tragically wrong." He could have been talking about today.

Danger surrounds us, and multi-threats to our security abound.

This is no time for a wobbly and wired-for-weakness commander-in-chief. As I study the candidates, I can't help but wonder how many smart people in this country will make a dumb choice for the next president again.

4/28/07

Let's look at Hillary

Three recent comments on the war in Iraq by Hillary Rodham Clinton as a candidate for the 2008 presidency need to be examined: 1. She will do all in her power to limit the "damage" by President Bush. 2. She "resents" Bush leaving the war on her desk if she becomes president. 3. She will end the war if elected. In 1952, General Dwight Eisenhower made a similar remark when he ran for president, "I will go to Korea" meaning he would end that war. Since then, we have had 55 years of war threat from North Korea, plus its acquisition of the atom bomb. This scenario sound familiar?

The Mideast threat has been churning for decades. Our past three presidents (Carter, Clinton, Bush) all weak and ineffective, fumbled opportunities by failing to take decisive action when confronted by crisis. The dangerous situation we find ourselves in today is a direct result of their timid responses.

Much can be attributed to our two-party system of government, and its inherent poverty of cooperation. A morbid dogma stamped eternal by Robert A. Taft, "Mr. Republican" during the 40's and 50's who said, "The purpose of the opposition is to oppose." Just how does this fulfill the rightful primary to serve the common good?

World War II and the Cold War had us on the brink of catastrophe. But we had leadership equal to the task. I do not see their equivalent capable of managing today's growing menaces at home and abroad. That includes Hillary. I do not say this with malice, of a lack of chivalry, but as a sensible and practical appraisal of her resume.

There is nothing in her term as Senator that sets her apart. She has been unproductive and has not authored meaningful legislation. She has not tasted the hard edges of worldwide statesmanship required for crisis management on a world stage. In my opinion, she is neither qualified nor worthy of the office of presidency. For the sake of history, and for the sake of future generations, we need a president (man or woman) who can command in the crucible of the moment. That is not Hillary.

9/15/07

Lay off Lieberman

To the Editor:

There is a measure of sweetness when voicing an opinion concerning people or events you disagree with. But there is a threshold where this sweetness becomes less endearing. And I find that the overabundance of opinion pieces and letters to the editor crushing the last measure of dignity out of U.S. Sen. Joe Lieberman crosses the threshold.

After the Los Angeles riots, precipitated by the Rodney King incident, syndicated columnist William Buckley wrote, "Whoa! Whoa! Whoa!" calling for an end the deluge of press opinions depicting the rioters as the aggrieved. "We don't condone this, but we understand," was the theme of most writers. Buckley wrote that the total immersion in one-sided arguments drowns recourse to balance and reason.

Like Mr. Buckley, I believe it is time to shout, "Whoa! Whoa! Whoa!" to bashing Lieberman. Like a drink to an alcoholic, one is too many and one hundred is not enough, especially when many letters reek of crassness that goes beyond politics and borders on personal attack. Just when does the echo chamber stop?

11/23/07

A feel good story

The country is aching for some good news. For a "feel good" story to offset the disturbing and divisive reports from Iraq, and the political street fighting in Washington, Mike Lupica, Sports Columnist for The New York Daily News, writes of the "lousiness that litters the landscape" of today's athletics. Well, if you watched the Boise State overtime win over Oklahoma in the Orange Bowl, we finally got that Christmas glow and New Year's cheer we desperately needed. The game contained the elements of David and Goliath, and the Prince Charming utopia of Cinderella and Snow White. The game tying "flea flicker" and the modernized version of the archaic "statue of Liberty" play routed the dark moods we have been besieged with. The first crocus appeared early, the blue bird sang out of season, and the baby smiled for the first time. And when the Boise State running back proposed to his cheerleader sweetheart on national TV, we all heard the echo of our own wedding bells. If you didn't walk away from that game "a most happy fella," with your insides warm and aglow, you better check your pulse. It took a bowl game to verify that revered Christmas fancy, "Yes, Virginia, there is a Santa Claus."

12/3/07

National leadership: where are we headed?

Great nations of history have been marked by great leadership. So have we in the early years as we struggled to define ourselves. Our founding fathers transcribed a constitution rooted in a foundation of faith, and designed to keep us politically pristine.

In the course of human events, basic assumptions of principled leadership emanated from the top. We have been blessed in that reality from Washington to Jefferson to Lincoln to Franklin Delano Roosevelt. Somehow, since then, we have lost our way. Nixon, Carter, Clinton, George W. Bush, political ineptness and moral weakness are their legacy.

Our two-party system bears the brunt of our nation's "fall from grace." Charisma, not character determines electability. Example: Bob Dole vs. Bill Clinton. Dole was a man of character, politically experienced, and a wounded WWII veteran. Clinton was a political neophyte, a notorious philanderer, but oozing charisma. Dole was considered dull, Clinton, charming, so he won. This is indicative of how our two-party system has blotted the honor and duty of governance for the common good.

Do you know the signature qualification for the presidency? It is to answer a question with such glibness, it leaves you dizzy. Charles Krauthamer, noted syndicated columnist, writes, "Washington, in recurring crises, with perfect regularity, is locked in utter predictability of bottomless cynicism." And George Schultz, former Secretary of State, said, "Nothing ever gets done in this town."

Old habits die hard, and we are growing old in our political sins. As old as the question Pontius Pilate asked Jesus, "What is truth?" This forecast the means of communication of all future politicians, and a main reason for today's voter apathy.

If we are to extricate ourselves from this political rubble, we must challenge and engage what former presidents Washington and Monroe foresaw as the "bane of our nation." The rubicon of our political salvation lies in a "Damascus moment"; the emergence with discipline and dignity to lead our country forward; to offer the little guy, "we, the people," a real chance to have our voices heard, and be truly represented. A third party with visionary leadership steeped in integrity, with ideas, direction, and purpose that will be lauded and supported by the public, whose welfare would be foremost. Is a third party realistic? Lowell Weicker did it. He became Governor of our state as a third party candidate in 1991.

12/6/07

Lieberman: provocateur or prophet

I say he is a prophet, but hear me out. As for being a provocateur, he means we need latitude in confronting treachery to protect our troops.

The unrelenting barrage of vehemence being rained on Senator Lieberman is becoming epochal. His recent advocacy for a military strike against Iran has raised a ferocious hostility that is way out of proportion to the occasion. It is a biting hatred whose depth of scurrility touches lunacy.

Disagree with him if you must, but he is right. There is proof of Iran's involvement of abetting insurgents in killing our troops in Iraq. But the focus of his call is the emerging nuclear threat, and Iran's stated intent to use it without equivocation.

In a recent article, syndicated columnist Charles Krauthamer writes about Iran's defiant development of its nuclear bomb, "We tremble because for the first time in history, nihilism will soon be armed with the ultimate weapon of annihilation. This gives him the means to match his ends." Osama Bin Laden trumps this with his majestic call to suicidal young, "It is wrong to love this world, die in the right cause, and go to the other world."

For my part, I believe Lieberman shows needed leadership in trying to awake us all to a greater conviction of what we face, and the vigilance we need to maintain in face of this threat.

12/15/07

Echoes of laptops at UConn

I have always believed that the University of Connecticut was an academic institution, and not the Department of Corrections. But a recent story in the Hartford Courant (12/16) about basketball recruit Nate Miles, stated, "Oft maligned teen may soon be in Storrs," challenges that assumption. Coach Calhoun considering a scholarship offer to this troubled youth with a long troubled past just lit up warning signs. Remember the stolen laptops and the coach's Twinkie resolution of layered hypocrisy and starchy morality on "not abandoning kids who get into trouble" especially if they are your ticket to a championship?

Reclamation projects are noble and commendable. But when that reclamation leads to a degree of tolerance for everything that is producing an unwillingness to restrict anything, then it is time to draw the line.

Follow the bouncing ball is not an approved remedial intervention for unacceptable behavior, and a university that provides sanction, crosses that threshold where it mortgages its soul for a piece of net. The coach is about to go there again, and he is allowed, because college athletics, like hogs, have been gorging at the money trough too long, that gate receipts trump academic integrity.

It doesn't have to be this way. Great universities are defined by how free they remain from scandal, especially in their athletic departments. Renowned university presidents demand this mandate. Myles Brand of Indiana fired basketball coach Bob Knight for habitual misconduct. Nancy Zimpher of Cincinnati did the same to coach Bob Huggins. Queasy ones at UConn expire in their silence and wet their pants.

12/18/07

Celebrity and the presidency

Before the Iowa caucus, Hillary Clinton was the odds-on-favorite to win the Democratic nomination, and was well on her way to becoming our first female president. But, Oprah's endorsement of Barack Obama added new political energy that has imploded the certainty of previous predictions.

The glitz and big bucks of celebrity endorsement always had its limitations. And Iowa State University political scientist Stephen Schmidt writes, "Most Americans are probably not going to let a celebrity tell them how to vote." Oprah's endorsement and the Iowa results challenge that assumption. She weaves a special magic, and her stumping for Obama was as devastating to Hillary's chances as tossing a fox into her hen house. Also, making her oft-claim, "I never think about losing," quite shaky, leaving the tracking polls in a shambles.

Oprah is center stage now, with the flash and power that makes one fall to the ground. It even has Obama wondering who is running,

Hillary was so sure of winning she took on her husband's "experience" mantra as her own. She assumed the unifying character of the sisterhood would never be breached. But Oprah's endorsement cut that Gordian knot, leaving her no longer the favorite.

Colin Powell was destined to become our first black president. He lost his chance, being duped by President Bush, to sell "weapons of mass destruction" to the United Nations that triggered a very unpopular war. Oprah now steps into the breach and passes the torch to Obama. It might work if she can subdue her intoxication of self-importance and remind herself who actually is running. Especially since the Iowa caucus results show America is tired of the Bill-and-Hill show, and is hungry for change, something new and refreshing. Can Oprah pull it off?

1/5/08

Bishop at war with the Advocate

To the Editor:

When given an opportunity to expand on his proclaimed policy of "transparency" by the Stamford Advocate, Bishop Lori declines and launches into an incongruous liturgy of spiritual unction's.

Had the Bishop acted timely and decisively when the scandal at St. John's in Darien surfaced, he could have avoided the ever-expanding clashes with the press and his parishioners. His ill-advised desire to keep it all hush-hush, private and secret has him entrapped and backed into a corner.

His failure to act with dispatch right from the start, has brought him the following consequences: an angry meeting with St. John parishioners where he was soundly castigated; the unjust punishment of a revered priest (Fr. Madden) which led to his resignation from the priesthood; and worst of all a no-end-sight pitch battle with the Advocate. The press accords no one, not even the Church, the right of a private existence, and the Bishop should be forewarned, nobody wins a war with the press. And I ask the Bishop, just where are we going with this?

Forgotten is the thieving, homosexual flaunting priest (Fr. Fay) who started all this. All the scamming from the diocesan office has allowed the culprit to enjoy the fruits of his crime. The harder the Bishop tries to defend his actions, the more he compounds an issue crying out for a resolution by simple and plain honesty. How I long to write laudably about my Bishop, but he exscinds that desire when he uses God as an accomplice in his cover.

1/21/08

Not "good priests"

In a February 12 letter, a writer takes the Advocate to task for its editorial citing Father Moynihan's de-frocking for financial mismanagement and cohabiting with his former music director (2/6). The writer praises Father Moynihan as a "good priest" for his "Christian caring work" as chaplain to cadets at the New York Maritime College, which he attended.

Bishop Bernard Law of Boston and Father Jude Fay of St. John's church in Darien were also called "good priests." They're now mired in scandal, forced to resign and one is going to prison. Before their fall, they gave great Sunday sermons, conducted spirit-enhancing retreats and charmed their parishioners with warm and glowing personalities. But, the charm masked their dark side.

What is soul-searing to me is the number of parishioners who laud and praise them for their "good works," but ignore their proven betrayal of their church community. Being so-called "good priests" does not mitigate the evil and harm they do.

Jesus warned us how convincing his false imitators can be. He railed against the unscrupulous priests of his time (Pharisees, Sadducees). When they tried to trap him with seditious questions (whose commands would we obey, yours or Caesar's?) he called them hypocrites and whited sepulchers full of dead men's bones.

Frauds and imposters are very adept at attracting the faithful to follow them into their fantasy world, until the deception disintegrates into painful disappointment. We are all subject to our passions, but misguided loyalty to wayward priests is not redemptive. Listen to what St. Paul has to say: "As I have said before, and now say again, if anyone preaches you a Gospel other than the one that you received, let that one be accursed."

2/15/08

Monsignor, blind to evil

Is it not the duty of a Pastor to confront evil menacing his flock, and to expose it resolutely? But, Monsignor Frank C. Wissel (Letter, 2/20) not only turns a blind eye to the ravages of Father Michael Moynihan, but renders approbation to this prodigal, thieving, fellow priest. The evil of Father Moynihan, like Father Jude Fay of St. John's Noroton, is gentrified by the rape of their parish treasuries of millions of dollars to finance the forbidden fruits of their sodomite lifestyle. What is it that beckons the good Monsignor to open himself to this travesty? Perhaps his wine deliveries should be curtailed.

The Monsignor also has a corkscrew obsession with "angry letter writers." He shoots his quiver full of arrows at his parishioners who file complaints against these priestly indiscretions. He lays an unworthy burden on them that traps him in his hypocrisy, because St. Thomas Aquinas writes, "When the faith is in imminent peril, prelates ought to be accused by their subjects, even in public."

In the Gospel of John (9:1-41) Jesus smears clay on a blind man's eyes and tells him to wash in the pool of Siloam, where his sight is restored. The Monsignor needs some of that clay applied to his eyes to remedy his spiritual blindness. The tone and texture of his letter violates the Divine order of his calling.

3/24/08

Unity 2008: the new politics

Do you know why we really need change in our national politics, because the simple virtue of telling the truth is absent? The honorable call to political service, to make the right decisions for the common good, has been vaporized by inter-party fratricide. Blinded by their anger and hatred of the opposition, Republicans and Democrats make a lot of noise about nothing. Out of the rubble, Cindy Sheehan and the New York Times rise to become the voice of the nation.

The great truth is that very little truth comes out of the political realm of our nation's capitol. The Gospel of anti-violence was born here, yet more violence to the truth is committed here than anywhere. Jesus always prefaced his remarks with "in very truth, I tell you." Arthur Schlesinger wrote "the truth that comes out of Washington, regardless of the party in power, is not a cure, but a dodge." This dishonesty has filtered into plagiarism by noted authors, and into resume writing. Michael Worthington, editor of "Resume Doctor" says "the broad implication of all this lying on job resumes, I see a society that's not valuing the truth." This truth twisting, wherever found, mutilates the spirit of our great nation, and renders dissolute the God- founded legacy of our historical beginnings.

A group of Wesleyan grads calling themselves "Unity 2008," have banded together to advocate a third party to challenge the long dominant two parties in power. Based on the premise that all citizens have reasonable expectations that the people they elect will transcribe the will of the people, they have set out on a course of change. The two-party system is like gum stuck to your shoe. No amount of scraping will eliminate it. It not only kills the messenger, it kills the message.

Noting the growing evidence that Americans are fed up with the ugly, unproductive partisan warfare served up by Republicans and Democrats, "Unity 2008" is determined to rise up and do something about it. The organizers plan to use college students and the Internet to mobilize millions of disappointed voters to nominate a third ticket, and engage the existing power structure.

The latest evidence that the public is disgruntled comes from a poll commissioned by organizers of "Unity 2008." It comes on top of scholarly research showing 74% of voters are dissatisfied with the way the country is going, and 72% say they would like a wider choice than just GOP and the Democrats. "Unity 2008" is sounding a call to action. If you count yourself among the voters growing disgusted with party lines, learn more about this movement and get involved.

5/15/08

Church calls on good Samaritans

Bishop William Skylstad of the Diocese of Spokane, Washington filed for Chapter 11 bankruptcy, and now needs $48 million to settle 177 claims of sexual abuse. He is asking his 82 parishes to donate $10 million to help bail him out. He runs God's and man's law in reverse: the victims to pay the fine for the criminals.

The real issue here is the spiritual bankruptcy of the many bishops who abetted the sexual abuse of children by priests under their watch, to burgeon themselves into this financial morass. Bishops who violated the fundamental principles of crisis management became thieves of the sacred.

Some parish priests are using the parable of the Good Samaritan to convince the faithful to contribute to the bail-out fund: "The Good Samaritan was not at all responsible for the problem." This constant plunder of verity leaves me dizzy. If Bishop Lori asked the parishioners of St. John's church in Noroton to replace the $1.4 million stolen by Father Jude Fay, under the pretext of the Good Samaritan, you would hear the roof blow off all the way to Oshkosh.

Bishop Skylstad himself is being accused of sexually abusing a woman when she was a student in the 60's. "I never broke my vow of chastity," he claims. He doesn't deny it, but invoking his chastity sets him free.

In conferring with learned people, deep into the study of church history and the evolution of the hierarchy, indicates it will take a generation before meaningful change abates the corruption. Meaning, the timeframe entrenched offenders get too old to rule, and we sweep away the wreckage of a dispirited church they leave behind.

Irreligious forces have their holiday in moments of great catastrophe. To expedite a quicker day of judgment, we need a profound Pontiff who will exercise the righteous anger of Jesus, and put the rope to the malefactors who desecrate His Father's House.

5/20/08

What is a hate crime?

The ruinous residual of slavery deserves condemnation. Civility dictates the time and place for remediation. But the 2008 presidential elections have brought this discourse to the level of effluvium.

I don't know the legal definition of a hate crime, but I know of people who used the "N' word were arrested and prosecuted. The Rev. Jeremiah Wright uses a national platform for his "Hate Whitey" demagoguery, which makes the "N" word seem like a marshmallow roast, and he is cheered. Just how do you wrap your mind around this racial divergence, one holy, one sinful?

Rev. Wright makes his special brand of racism a religion. Obama played a soft shoe apostle until the volcano erupted, and the fallout threatens his once sure presidency. He is learning as in <u>The Ancient Mariner</u>, albatrosses can become quite burdensome.

Black allegiance is no mystery. Al Sharpton and Jesse Jackson: there rivalry smolders in private. But in egregious commitance by either, they cover for each other publicly. So, why is Rev. Wright making a train wreck of Obama's presidential aspirations? Why has he become an obstacle to the possibility of Obama becoming the first black president? The only ones to benefit are the white candidates whose very thought sets his tail on fire.

His "Damn America" vitriol smolders like a nascent volcano, whose hate-filled eruptions bury all in its path. They make the earth tremble and bring your house down. For Obama, it is his run for the White House which he had in his grasp, which is coming down…And out of the rubble, here come Hil and Bill singing, "Show me the way to go home."

5/30/08

The firing of a president

This country has a long history of war. That history continues as we are engaged in war in distant lands of Afghanistan and Iraq. Knocking down our twin towers on 9/11 is justification of our troops being in Afghanistan. It is in response to that enormous evil perpetrated by Osama Bin Laden. The invasion of Iraq remains questionable. Five years and little measurable progress is bringing on wholesale disillusionment. And many voices are calling for retreat.

Causes are forgotten when rising casualties become the focus, abetted by a hostile press and slanted media; compounded when objectives are not clearly defined. From a rising chorus of partisan rigidity, come comments that the lives of the brave and gallant troops are being "wasted," and the war is lost. This is irresponsible and excretal party bilge.

There is an old saying, "When you lose a war you fire the general." After Pearl Harbor, we not only fired a general (Walter Short), but also an admiral (Husband Kimmel). Daily news reports indicate that for the first time in our history, we are about to fire a president. George Washington suffered his "Iraqi" moment at Valley Forge. Can you imagine the consequences if he was fired then? James Madison, after his ill-advised War of 1812, convinced him that unbridled executive power, especially in the time of war, posed a great threat to the cause of republic government.

In wars dark moments, history tells us blame must fall somewhere. All fingers usually point to the man at the top. Perhaps President Bush is experiencing Madison's prognostication of the crippling effect of the excess of power.

We all long for a "feel good" ending to this war. I want to believe what Bush said at Arlington on Memorial Day, "They know this war will end one day, as all wars do. Our duty is to ensure that its outcome justifies the sacrifices made by those who fought and died in it." This sounds like a commander-in-chief finding his way back.

Our republic was born to break away from the familial ascendency of monarchy. In our continuing experiment of government by self-rule, keeping the presidency in the family has proven a bad precedent. If

Hillary is elected president, inheritance by family will continue. This is not in the best interest of a nation desperately needing change and new leadership.

5/31/08

Can Obama win with the Devil on his back?

Barack Obama just pulled the greatest political upset since Truman beat Dewey in 1948. His call for "change" promises to put 20 years of rule by the Clintons and the Bush's in the rear view mirror. But there is an old saying, "It is hard to dance with the Devil on your back": the Reverends Wright and Pfleger, and Bill Ayers, a domestic terrorist, and Chicago pal Tony Rezko, facing 20 years for fraud and soliciting bribes.

As the Hippies gone mad stormed off our campuses to excise America of its warts, Bill Ayers and Bernadine Dohrn led the radical Weather Underground, who preferred to bomb America back to Utopia. Time restored the rule of law. Ayers dodged prison, and now pirates respectability as a professor at the University of Chicago. Not surprising, as academia, in its superior Jeffersonian intellect sanctify themselves. Here he has become a cozy friend and political collaborator of Obama.

Rod Dreher, Dallas Morning News editorial columnist, in an Advocate Op/Ed (5/18) writes, "Know why the domestic terrorist team of Ayers and Dohrn never went to jail? The FBI broke so many laws trying to catch them, putting them on trial would have been futile." From his academic sanctuary, in his pustular pride, he boastfully regrets, "We didn't plant enough bombs." This is a razor's edge from anarchy.

When George Washington left office, he said, "the political world has changed, and parties, not great men, would soon become the objects of contention." You delude yourself if you think the presidency is won on merit. Power brokers of enormous wealth wield enormous influence. They pull the strings attached to the man they put in the oval office. If you seek grace, go to church on Sunday.

Leadership is born in the crucible of adversity. Obama made a flimsy response during his baptism of fire during the Rev. Wright firefight. How much armor will he bring to his first debate with John McCain? Slick dismissals and foggy-bottom answers over Ayers and Rezko ("it was a bonehead move") will not set him free. This is where the fruits of campaign rhetoric die on the vine. The flash and power of Obama's oratory is said to make one fall to the ground. I heard it said he can talk a cat out of a tree. With this Devil on his back, can he talk McCain out of the presidency?

6/10/08

Resiliency of Joe Lieberman

The Apaches practiced the "Ghost Dance" around their campfires, believing it would make them bullet proof when they faced the cavalry. I don't know what dance Joe Lieberman struts, but the full force of the Democratic party "shock and awe" finds him still standing.

The frequency and virulence of their anti-Lieberman crusade, needs to be engaged, if just for the sake of balance. Hillary canonized herself but got a free pass. Obama's new-age politics of "change" is looking much like the same old wrinkles, and gets a few winks. The Democrats pinned Joe Lieberman to a Velcro wall, but he pulled himself free and beat them. He is now free-wheeling to a greater position of importance. This is what drives a never ending stream of bile and denunciations from within his party.

The Democrats were overjoyed when Lieberman was defeated in the senatorial primary. But you don't turn the lights out until the "fat lady sings." In the end, she sang for Joe, making him stickier than raw rubber for them.

Mr. Lieberman has had his political blind spots. He did not tip-toe his way to senatorial leadership. He has been in the trenches and is battle tested. The unremitting attacks for his support of John McCain show he is a rare political breed who divests the party yoke, for a firmly held set of principles. The truth is the Democrats need him more than he needs them.

The ferocity of an animal increases when it is backed into a corner and needlessly taunted. Urban people who never had a rural experience are ignorant of this. Many life lessons come hard.

Some of the best stories ever written begin with this tantalizing query, "Get out of Dodge by sundown." (Remember High Noon?) This call is being issued by Howard Dean, High Sheriff of Donkeytown. No matter how many guns they bring, betcha Joe Lieberman will not be on that stagecoach.

7/25/08

Goodbye steaks

Spurred by Al Gore's book, <u>An Inconvenient Truth</u>, climatology is becoming a new religion. For ecological mandarins, global warming is becoming a greater threat than radical Islam terrorism. They are especially obsessed with the effects of cow flatulence on the climate. They claim unless we control the passing of gas by our cows, the polar ice cap will melt.

The cattle ranchers are being besieged to take immediate curative action. But nobody is offering any preventive measures. This is not like curbing smoking. How do you inhibit a cow from performing his natural digestive process?

The climatologists are offering this suggestion that ranchers herd their cows into specially constructed sheds to capture the gas they emit (methane) in special containers where it will be used to generate electricity. Impractical, implausible, and overly expensive, say the ranchers. It changes their industry from beef production to vapor chasers and emission canners.

Like the protection conferred on the snail darter, that impeded flood control projects, the watch dog environmentalists threaten the extinction of our steaks, our briskets, our prime rib, our roasts, our stews and our burgers. Move over vegetarians.

9/8/08

Russell is right

To the editor:

Don Russell, in his column (10/15) "we need to cast an informed vote," in an insightful dissection of how and why our election process has become perverted, and how, we as voters, can overcome, as he puts it, "the cacophony of verbiage that swills from the media." To determine our vote, we really need to know the abilities and sound judgment of whom we choose to run this great nation; who proposes the most sound solutions and courses of actions to the many pressing problems our country faces. Mr. Russell advises that voters need to scrutinize and study the candidates' history, service records, and their contributions in legislating sound policies during their tenure in political office.

The nation seems to judge candidates by their rankings in the polls. But former President Harry Truman said of polls, "I wonder how far Moses would have gone if he took a poll on Egypt."

Much of the pronouncements from both camps are slur contests of name calling, replete with half-truths. Most half-truths are worse than a lie. Yet, this is the perversion of our election process of which Mr. Russell writes.

George Washington, when he left office, foresaw the "fall from grace" in our future presidential elections, when he said, "Parties, not great men, have now become the objects of contention.

He is right. History shows partisan rancor and rule by discord has extended into the McCain-Obama election.

Mr. Russell reminds us with the elevating crises we face at home and abroad, we must demand better from our government. The man we choose to lead us must be the measure of a studied and informed vote.

10/18/08

Election post-mortem

I feel inadequate to join the giants of journalism in their lofty full-page editorials, dissecting the recent presidential election. My post-mortem is simple. John McCain could not avoid the posse chasing this Republican administration out of town. It is hard to dance with the devil on your back, and McCain had Bush and Cheney on his. In spite of these odds, which indicated a Barry Goldwater-like drubbing, the "old warrior" garnered remarkable numbers (56 m or 46% of the popular vote). This is not an overwhelming mandate. Consider, McCain was leading in early September, but the market crashed, which proved to be the lance that fatally pierced his side.

What I find most disturbing, is the media lynching of Sarah Palin. In a shark-like feeding frenzy, a hostile press sniffed under frozen moose chips, to unearth meaningless flaws. To me, she was as fresh as new fallen snow amid the arena of lock-jawed political hustle.

Our country is still evolving. It was inevitable that someday we would elect our first black or woman president. The suspension of certainty of that historical moment has come. The people have spoken. Regardless of our sentiments, now is the time for all of us to rally behind our newly elected president, who faces a prodigious task of cleaning up the mess he has inherited.

11/12/08

Cheers for Hillary and Holder

Did anybody notice that the market endured the fourth worst drop ever for the Dow (680 points) on the day of Hillary's nomination for Secretary of State, and Eric Holder for Attorney General was made? The market usually rebounds when favorable political announcements are made. Short memories entwine political incongruity. But let's give Hillary a pass until her pant suits turn to mix and match. Remember the Gospel by Bubba: 2 for the price of 1? Well, he's back so that Washington stirs and the interns tremble. Let me point out that many people become hard of hearing, when I mention the Clintons personify a remarkable disrespect for the moral dimension of leadership.

Eric Holder was deputy Attorney General who made the key sanction for Bubba to grant a pardon to Marc Rich. Mr. Rich was a fugitive commodities trader who fled to Switzerland to avoid prosecution for 65 counts of tax evasion. Bubba is about to release a list of donors to his foundation (part of the deal in Hillary's appointment). Check to see how heavily Mr. Rich and his former wife Denise have contributed.

Richard Cohen, noted political Columnist, writes in the New York Daily News, "Holder was involved in just the sort of inside- the- Belt influence peddling that our newly elected president promised to end." And the beat goes on. Just as former president Ronald Reagan used to say, "There you go again."

Over the phone, I've been told many times to "quit nit-picking." I will when our elected officials cut the corn, and give it to us straight, because integrity and trust is never negotiable when they stop alienating the truth that binds us to the common good.

12/4/08

Blue eyes

I've been asked many times if there is a story of merry tidings amongst my usual chomp and stomp. Yes, there is, and I'm sure you will like it.

While attending a UConn football game at Storrs, with my wife, on the way out we were approached by a small group of overly excited women (my wife still claims I paid them) asking if I was Paul Newman. My blue eyes and signature cap can do this, as it has happened before. I could not autograph their programs, nor could I convince them they were mistaken. They persisted, drawing an unwanted audience as we exited the stadium. Finally realizing my wife did not resemble Joanne Woodward, they left.

This letter is to commend newly elected Repesentative Jim Himes for co-sponsoring a House resolution (Advocate, January 1) to honor Mr. Newman for his humanity and charitable largesse.

Join my wife and me in being contributors to the Hole in the Wall Gang Camp, a special residential camp for children with dire medical conditions, built especially to serve them by Mr. Newman. You will feel good about yourself, and better about Mr. Newman's legacy, and Mr. Himes, above political thoughtfulness. Does this merit a star?

01/21/09

Handling bullies

The ancient Greeks gave us democracy and knowledge and culture and wisdom and philosophy and war as redeeming qualities. Aristotle said, "You must live life forward, but you can only understand it backward."

Let me take you backward to my time. A time of the Great Depression, and that Great War, of which I helped write a chapter. To my hometown (Middletown), and my high school days (1939 – 43), and the bully I engaged.

The insidious infiltration of school bullies has been long and constant. Like an alcoholic, one shove is too many and 100, not enough. They suck the life out of what should be a memorable school experience for many students.

Let me tell you about our remedy. Our bully was named "Smitty" L., menacing, snarling, hulking. He'd push us smaller kids around, stuff us into lockers, toss our books down the hallways. We were tough neighborhood kids who could handle ourselves with equals. But engaging the bully in a fist fight? Our reason subdued our courage, as the cost would be too great.

One of our crowd was "Jumbo" J., – a tough farm kid and a match for the bully. We didn't hide behind him, but we called him when we needed help. We lived by the code, "In the alley after school, there just ain't no golden rule." So one day after school, Jumbo applied this code to Smitty. We were never bullied again. Won't work today in this insanely litigious society, the bully is favored. You end up on the wrong end of a suit.

There is an epilogue to this story. I left school early to join the Navy. On leave from boot camp, I went to see my class graduate. After the war, I reported to Pier No. 92, after a 30-day leave then transferred to the Brooklyn Navy Yard to serve my last two months. In the chow line one day, someone grabbed me in a bear hug with the warmest greetings. It was Smitty, the former bully. The uniform made us equals. On weekends, we rode the train home together. He insisted I had to have supper at his house one evening. He said his mother's pasta was the best I'd ever taste. He was right.

We would run into each other after we were discharged; have a few beers, and be the best of friends. We still are. Here's to Smitty and Jumbo and a happy ending to a bully story. How did others end?

02/24/09

When stewards become vandals

The authors of the Constitution left us a message that political service is for the good of all and in union with the will of the people. Where has this stewardship gone? Here are some examples where the stewards became vandals: Charles Rangel, Tom Daschele, Tim Geithner, Nancy Killefer, all exposed as tax cheats. Chris Dodd abrogates his oversight responsibility as chairman of the Banking Committee by availing himself of subprime mortgages that ignited our financial collapse. These are blistering displays of parasitic ironies, facades of political purity, who grub for advantage. By repeated re-election they give themselves an immunity to navigate the darkness. When exposed, the brethren adjourn to the Capitol lounge, and over cocktails out-snicker each other, equating themselves to schoolchildren getting caught tossing spitballs in the classroom.

There was a time when we as a nation stood fully confident in the worthiness of our causes. Our leaders were dedicated servants of the public. They had national appeal – grace, trust, quiet courage – to muster the productive enterprise to contribute to the common good. Just name one upon whom we can pin a star, as I want to stand up and cheer.

Where are the venerable watchdogs who use the measure of law to keep order and everyone on an acceptable plateau of virtue? The ugly reality is the depth and magnitude of wrongdoing in high office is being tolerated with a wink and a shrug.

Insider politics, like insider trading, ordains the rot that bleeds across our headlines and TV screens. The latest shooting stars are Bernard Madoff and Gov. Blagojevitch. Both would lead us to the fountain, but it is like drinking from a fire hose.

There is a noticeable absence of high regard for our elected officials. Public explanations of their wrong doing are effusive bromides that become a crisis of the truth.

It starts when they mistake the mud of the Potomac for the Rubicon, then stretch the boundaries of their limits, and never find their way back.

Harry Truman, after his first day in the Senate, said, "What am I doing here?" A year later he said, "What are they doing here?"

Times were hard when I was young. After a long day of complaining, my father took me to the local pub and said, "Everything looks rosy after a few stiff drinks." Thanks Pop.

03/30/09

Miles was wrong for UConn

There is a Biblical saying that a prophet is honored everywhere except in his hometown. Well, on December 25, 2007, the Advocate printed a letter I wrote ("Calhoun goes down dangerous road") predicting dire consequences in his recruitment of Nate Miles, a troubled but very talented basketball player. It didn't take long as Miles was expelled from the University for harassing a female student.

Coach Calhoun prides himself as a Father Flanagan, administering Boy's Town style of discipline to his errant players. Remember the stolen laptops? It cuts him enough slack to keep one step ahead of the posse.

Recent revelations (and they keep on growing) of recruitment violations of Miles by Calhoun, former coach Tom Moore and other related team personnel has set off the NCAA dogs baying, are about to bite them all right in the gluteus.

04/12/09

Bishop's folly

The rumble at the state capitol, led by Bishop Lori, posing as Richard the Lionhearted leading his crusaders to besiege the infidels, was not a spiritual mission. It was all about control of diocesan wealth. Bishops constantly warn us about the hazards of poverty as they pass the Sunday basket. But Jesus warned us about the spiritual hazards of wealth. Waving his sword, the Bishop snookered his flock into believing the protest was about the usurpation of religion. The faith of our fathers was not stolen. Our money was stolen. Stolen by priests the Bishop should have been watching. The losses were in the millions, and in so many years, you have to ask, just what was he watching?

In the Lenten season of repentance, the Bishop is supposed to lead the faithful in prayer, fasting, and works of mercy, chasing Beelzebub out of town, not the money tree all the way to Hartford. The truth is, he was conveniently purblind when the thefts by his homosexual priests were on a thieves' holiday. When finally exposed, he turned into a wrathful reformer, double-locking the vault after it was emptied. This does not meet the standards of vigilant safekeeping.

The church is better served by one crusading Tom Gallagher and the much maligned Voice of the Faithful, than a hundred pusillanimous bishops. The mission of the church, as ordained by Jesus Christ, needs no political hack rallies, disguised as a morality play. Providing a remedy for sinners is hard to do when occupied with keeping the books. Or, was it his immersion in prayerful retreat that caused his lax oversight of his priests that allowed the thievery and the rampant sodomite hi-jinks in the rectories to continue right under his spectacles?

Rallying his flock to storm law-makers, shouting "CRUCIFY," surely inspired some zealots to issue deadly threats to the two sponsoring legislators. The fall-out also caused one of the Irish legislators to withdraw from marching in the St. Patrick's Day parade in his hometown. When do we resume burning at the stake?

4/15/09

Tears for Kent State

Recent Advocate article (4/27): "Police Fire on Kent State Rioters," awakened some sad memories for me. Soon after the summer of 1970 National Guard killing of four rioting students, I attended a National YMCA Certifying Workshop for Test and Measurements of physical fitness on that campus. It was designed to provide the latest safe and effective training techniques to advance cardio-vascular health, and how to measure that progression and advancement.

It was held in early September, before the return of the student body. We stayed in the dorm and ate with the football team. Athletic dorms and dining areas are usually wild, loud, playful, and raucous. Not this time. It was a graveyard atmosphere: solemn, morbid, grieving. Even our usual YMCA camaraderie and fellowship was subdued into an exhausted decorum. The campus, under tight security, it was difficult applying ourselves to the task at hand, or reconciling the blanket doom that was everywhere. The head football coach was so distraught he resigned before the first game.

Kent State University is aesthetic and renowned. Usually a delight to visit, but no matter the place; no matter the time; no matter the cause; rioting and shooting our students on our campuses make us all less human. I know. I've been there.

4/28/09

Second guessing the president

I like Mike Lupica and his style of sports writing, but when he tries his hand as a war correspondent, I find him wanting. He bases his viewpoint (New York Daily News, 5/10) on a simple interview with a soldier facing a second tour of duty to Iraq.

To understand the war in Iraq takes depth and breadth of Mideast history, a complex and complicated series of events requiring intelligent and scholarly analysis. Even lifelong political diplomats of foreign-service are confounded.

Explaining the war is difficult enough, and it has its roots in the country's history. Iraq, formerly Babylonia, was a fertile, verdant, rich land, with two great rivers. Many believe it was the location of the Garden of Eden. The wheel and writing were invented there. The capital city was the center of mathematics, music and culture, and one of the Seven Wonders of the World: the Hanging Gardens of Babylon; sometimes called the "cradle of civilization."

Many great military powers (Greeks, Persians, Roman Empire) invaded to steal the rich fruits of the land, even Alexander, the Great. But, just like today, the insurgents rose up to drive the invaders away. What is chiseled in my mind is the mournful epithet, "the bones of the conquerors were left to bleach in the hot desert sand."

I wonder how much of this preamble has Mike Lupica studied. An interview with a soldier falls far short. I myself do not know how the "surge" of additional troops by President Bush will turn out. But I do know the jury is still out on the outcome of the war, and we should not interfere with the verdict. I am just being studious so I do not wish to offend Mr. Lupica. But I will relay to him what my history professor always said to me whenever I came up short, "Mr. Gawlak, 'foggy bottom' answers will not do in my class."

5/12/09

Cigar memories

I need to comment on Mark Drought's Viewpoint article (April 24) concerning the changing policy on the Cuban embargo. But his comments on Cuban cigars more than tickled my nicotine nefariousness. I have a long history with tobacco farming and the cigar industry.

During the Great Depression, from age 14 to 16, I worked in the tobacco fields along the Connecticut River. That was a time when tobacco was considered a wholesome product and was used with sophistication. A major motion picture about the tobacco industry ("Parrish," featuring Troy Donahue) was filmed here on location in 1961.

When school let out, Consolidated Cigar Co. would truck us to the fields and return us at day's end. We worked nine-hour days for 25 cents an hour. The tobacco was shade- grown, cultivated under huge fields of white netting.

Picking tobacco was delicate agriculture and required special training. A mercurochrome marker on the inside of your forearm measured the correct length of the leaf to be picked. A special technique was required to keep from tearing the leaf. When brought to the shed, the leaves were put in bundles and hoisted above to be dried by charcoal fire pots. Occasionally, a shed (they were as big as a football field) would catch on fire. There were spectacular blazes, especially at night.

When I turned 17, I joined the Navy, and my cigar history followed me. At a ship's store, you could buy a box of White Owls for 50 cents. While at anchor and the smoking lamp was lit after working hours, the crew would gather on the fantail or up in the gun tubs to relax until lights out. Smoking or playing pinochle was the usual. You could gamble down in the sail locker, but it meant brig time if you got caught.

Age was no factor being in "this man's Navy," so the "old salts" expected you to light up to show your toughness. I had difficulty hiding my dizziness and often had to go below to recover. There wasn't much laughter as we headed up the line, but my posturing bravado to snooker a veteran crew provided some.

Home after the war, I would celebrate weddings, birthdays,

graduations, and anniversaries with a Rosedale or a Ramon Allanos. The White Owls we smoked aboard ship were "ropes" by comparison.

This brings me to the essence of Mr. Drought's article. Being a cigar smoker, he can't wait to taste a premium Cuban cigar. I assume he is referring to a Cohiba at $25.00 a pop, too pricey and dicey for me.

All of this cigar talk reminds me of my two favorite quotes: "There are two things a man never forgets – his first love and his first cigar," by John Bain. And this by Mark Twain: "If I cannot smoke my cigar in Heaven, then I shall not go."

Do you know that most presidents, after a trying day, relaxed by smoking a good cigar?

06/07/09

Strong-willed generation

George Bernard Shaw wrote, "Youth is wasted on the young." This is an enigma to my generation (Great Depression, WWII) and I can't let this pass. While downy days were few, growing up during the Great Depression, we engaged our struggles and took command of the moment. Here are some anecdotes about a boy, a river, and coming of age.

Growing up on the Connecticut River during these trying times, I swam, fished and hunted those waters. This was not for sport, but as a supplemental source of sustenance. The river teemed with fish and the game, in the surrounding woods were abundant. You acquired the natural stealth of your quarry, and matched wits.

To catch fish, you studied their feeding habits and choice of bait. This was central to my success to bringing to the table trout, calico bass, pike, perch, and shad. The woods supplied squirrels, rabbits, pheasants, partridge and deer. We were amused by inedible raccoons, skunks, possum, woodchucks and foxes dashing to their dens. Partridge were our greatest challenge. Their evasive tactics and drumming wings kept you off balance. They made the tastiest meals as they fed on wild berries. Wild game was tangy, and cooking required much garnishing.

Bald eagles reigned. Their beauty, grace, and majesty kept you mesmerized as they plucked fish or ducks from the river with the deftness of a thief. The lead on flying ducks was gauged by their distance and speed. These calculations served me well when I became part of a 40mm anti-aircraft gun crew aboard ship during the war.

The river nestled in the valley, and sound was magnified as it echoed hither and yon. It made the cawing of a flock of crows aggravating. Startling plunges of ospreys and kingfishers brought you to a start. A water snake slithering by with a struggling frog, and a 60 pound snapping turtle laying her eggs in the sand was nature in the raw. We brought home pails of wild blackberries, raspberries, and blueberries. The pies my mother baked were not the jell-filled morass you get in today's market. How I long for the original.

The river became risky in winter and spring. Severe cold capped the river in ice 2 feet thick. Coast Guard cutters kept the channel open for coal and fuel barges which re-froze quickly after they passed. On a dare we would dash across as if playing hop-scotch on burning coals. Ice jams would make the channel impassable and were dynamited into spectacular plumes of ice shards, smoke and water. Melting snows and heavy rains in spring would bring the river to flood stage. It became a muddy, surging ribbon of debris and destruction which did not recede until early June.

With the passing years, it is time that steals from us. Yet, the river never changes. I still go back to visit. For I follow the rhyme of the poet who reminds us, all roads lead home.

6/20/09

Lies, lies, lies

One day, Bernard Madoff called his two sons into his office and informed them the incredible success of his investment firm was "one big lie." Wow, was it! It cost him 150 years in prison.

Do you know where lying started? Adam blamed Eve, and the creature blamed his envy. The master said, "Liar, liar, fig leaf on fire," and banned them east of Eden, where their progeny elevated their fragility to a new level, which continues today.

Cain slew his brother and said he was not responsible. Moses played god drawing water from a rock. Judas gave the most infamous kiss of them all. It took a flash of lightning to set St. Paul straight. Richard the Lionhearted told Saladin to get out of Jerusalem by sundown. Brutus killed his best friend because he was too ambitious.

Let's skip the small stuff and get to the juice. FDR said the WPA and the CCC camps would get us out of the depression. Pshaw! It took a war. Dewey said, 'I won," while Truman laughed. Nixon said," I'm not a crook." When asked about Iran Contra, Reagan said, "No way." JFK said," I and Marilyn are just pals." Bill Clinton said," I did not have sex with that woman." Bush saw weapons of mass destruction in a vision, while Dodd said, "what mortgages?" Ted Kennedy related what a tough swim Chappaquiddick was, and O.J. is diligently searching for his wife's killer on the golf course. With Al Sharpton, Tawana Brawley, Jesse Jackson and his secretary's phantom pregnancy? Am I glad to hear the secret of Roger Clemens's and Barry Bonds' new way to build muscle. Push weights like hell. Aren't these beauts?

I have to mention some brave hearts who did not lie. Lee told Grant, "You beat me." Wyatt Earp said, "Meet me at the O.K. Corral," and Sitting Bull told Custer, "Stay out of my yard." John Wayne told everyone, "Get out of my way."

When I was 17, I forged my father's name to my enlistment papers when I joined the Navy. When the recruiter asked if it was authentic, I swore to a lie.

George Orwell said, "Political language is to make all lies sound truthful." Now there are little white lies and whoppers. Which ones do you use?

7/10/09

Lighter Side of the news

With daily accounts of healthcare reform, our local political races for mayor, and Governor Rell's embattled accounts form Hartford, politics is the cachet of our news. Let us go to the lighter side.

Richard Poncher, a "serial entrepreneur," who built two bullet proof cars for Al Capone, is buried in the crypt above Marilyn Monroe. He bought the crypt from Joe Dimaggio, when the Yankee great was in the midst of his divorce from Monroe. On his deathbed, Richard ordered his wife, Elsie, "When I croak and you don't put me upside down over Marilyn, I'll haunt you the rest of your life'. Playboy's Hugh Hefner, bought the crypt next to Monroe. Word is out he wants to be buried on his side facing Marilyn.

Early American literature is laced with tales of "noble savages." Is there no escape?

10/21/09

Cheaters as role models

Public trust in government tumbled to a new low in Stamford (Advocate, 10/16) during a Democratic fund raiser: President Obama raised the triumphant hand of Senator Chris Dodd, not as a corrupt sinner, but as a saint. Just how do you control your anger when you see misconduct in office celebrated instead of castigated?

Politics is the strange religion where grievous sin is for the opposition. Confessions, admission of guilt, contrition are flaked off as minor errors of judgment.

Where did we go wrong as a nation? What has happened to a watchdog press eager to expose the dark side of humanity? The old Chicago Daily News instructed all of their beat reporters, "If your mother tells she loves you, check it out." Yet, the New York Times, during the eight year term of President Bush, acted as a private public relations firm in the employ of the Democratic Party.

Stigma in sports is erased with the next home run or touchdown. In politics, all is forgiven with raising the hand of a candidate in the winner's circle. When does President Obama lead the pep-rally for Charles Rangel? And I hope Senator Dodd has enough Ben-Gay to assuage his aching back from joyous pounding.

Former U.S. Senate Chaplain Edward Everett Hale was asked, "Do you pray for the Senators, Dr. Hale?" "No, I look at the senators and pray for the country."

10/31/09

The odyssey of campaign rhetoric

The central dynamic of presidential campaign rhetoric is defined as million dollar promises but ten cent fulfillment. It is these false promises that foster election, but lead to destabilization of the problem discussed (in this case, war). Listen to what Barack Obama promised if elected president, "I will bring the troops home in six months." Reality, he is sending 30,000 more troops over there. This is not a draw down but escalation. After listening to dozens of Cinderella solutions during the past election, I wrote in this paper on 11/26/06, "Be careful what you ask for."

We are seeing the forefront of advances in the Obama administration: conflict resolution over a few beers; and now the indemnification of 9/11: holding the trial of the main perpetrator, Khalid Shaith Mohammed in a civil court in New York City.

Syndicated columnist Charles Krauthamer calls it, "Gratuitously granting him the greatest propaganda platform from which to proclaim the glory of jihad and the criminality of infidel America." This is distilling the debate to its essentials. In its simple facticity, it enters the realm of fantasy, impoverishes human reasoning, because it is being stage managed.

When you use tropes that trap, you disengage first principles that become vacuous rationale. Listen to Attorney General Eric Holder defending his decision, "to enlighten the world to the superiority of our system where the rule of law and fair trial reigns." When asked, "What happens when KSM and his co-defendants do not get convicted?" he replied, "Failure is not an option." Isn't this what we heard at the trial of O.J. Simpson? I find this stultifying rather than resolving. How say you?

11/29/09

Pearl Harbor and Five Brothers

The attack on Pearl Harbor 68 years ago would send five brothers to war and leave a profound and memorable effect. My older brother, Stan, joined the Navy three months before and was stationed on a cruiser in Boston. Two days after the attack, still grimy from loading ammunition, he came home on a 24 hour leave to tell us he was shipping out the next day. My three older brothers were soon drafted, and we would not see each other until the war ended. Two would serve in the European theatre fighting their way across North Africa, then up the Italian peninsula. The other two and myself would island hop across the vast South Pacific. We would miss seeing each other by a narrow margin.

I was 15 on December 7, 1941; too young to comprehend the geography and the consequences. A year and a half later, I would also join the Navy. Home from "Boots," I would watch my high school class graduate. Shipping out of San Francisco on a transport, we would stop at Pearl. A solemn silence prevailed as we passed the sunken U.S.S. Arizona. The blackened super-structure had been removed. All that remained above sea level were the round gun mounts upon which rests today's memorial.

At New Caledonia, I would board my ship, the U.S.S. Whitney, and head for Guadalcanal where the island hopping began. The island was secure except for the frequent bombing raids upon Henderson Field.

As the campaign progressed north, I would just miss seeing two of my brothers: Paul, with First Cavalry in the Admiralty Islands north of New Guinea; and Stan in the Philippines aboard the heavy cruiser, USS Vincennes. Paul's outfit pulled out the day before. Stan's ship was getting underway as we approached and were warned to "lay off" as a quad 40 mm swung around to take aim at our motor launch. Navy protocol warns you do not approach a man-of-war when the gangway is up.

We were in Leyte Gulf when the war ended, gearing up to join the occupation forces in Tokyo Bay. Veteran crew was offered the option to stay with the ship or head home. We couldn't pack fast enough. On a transport stateside, it was 21 days of pinochle, chow lines, flying fish, and dreaming of home. Finally the warm glow of seeing the Golden Gate Bridge shrouded in fog.

Having served four years, my older brothers were already home, some wounded, all highly decorated. Being the youngest, I was the last to come home. As I came through the door, my brother Joe jokingly said, "What took you so long?" Talking like a rebel and wearing an earring, my father was puzzled at the changes in his youngest. He asked Joe why "Yosh" talked so funny, and what was that in my ear?" He was told, "Forget it, Pop, he's gone Asiatic." Homecoming was a nightly gathering at the local pub celebrating their kid brother who made it back.

All the brothers are gone now. They sleep in honored glory of noble warriors which will always be their Pearl Harbor legacy.

12/9/09

Loss of a unique friend

My five year old grandson Charlie was helping me clear the yard of branches caused by a recent wind storm. Out in the middle of the road was a squirrel apparently run over by a car. Upon close examination, it turned out to be the one-eyed squirrel I wrote about in this newspaper (July 19, 2004). I knew it was him by a distinctive identifying mark (a nick in his left ear).

He wasn't quick enough to outmaneuver the other squirrels and birds for the nuts I fed them. So he would come to the back porch and pitter patter with his paws on the storm door. I also knew he was there by the low guttural squawk of a scolding daw berating him.

As I gathered the remains for disposal, my grandson said, "Grandpa, he didn't look both ways." This was the cautionary admonition he was always given before crossing the street.

When you become attached to an animal (wild or pet) its death can rival the passing of a family member. We had to put down two pet cats because they became terminally ill with old age. As I took them to the veterinarian I am still haunted by the sobs and tears of the children and grandchildren. I left it to my wife to do the consoling.

Pets are easily replaced. Just how do you replace an adopted, loveable one-eyed squirrel, who trundles sideways, has part of his ear missing, knocks on your door when he's hungry, and doesn't look both ways when crossing the street? Do you have a better children's fable?

1/18/10

The lore of the crow

The New York Daily News (1/18) carried a photo of a red hawk dislodged from his roost by a clutter of crows. My yard and neighborhood has been inundated by large gatherings of crows. Their numbers have multiplied ten-fold and have become a nuisance and a curiosity. They fill the treetops, roofs, and cover the ground pecking and feeding. They are not easily disturbed and only take flight when approached. I grew up along the Connecticut River and have a long history with crows, sometimes compatible and sometimes nemesis.

Growing up during the Depression, we all hunted game to supplement the dinner table. Wild ducks, pheasants, partridge, rabbits and squirrels were plentiful. Crows were everywhere, but considered a nuisance. They were wary and cagey, and very adept at keeping themselves out of harm's way. The flock protected themselves by placing a lone sentry at a safe distance who would sound the alarm as hunters approached. Then, the flock would break out in a cawing ruckus that agitated both humans and animals. This agitation was the only reason we would try to bring them down, since they were inedible.

Lore has it, that in late fall, a very large number of crows would gather deep in the forest to hold court. Judgment was to be passed on a lone member who transgressed against the code of behavior. If found guilty, the flock would descend on the perpetrator, peck his eyes and most of his feathers out in a cawing frenzy, then would turn the sky black as they dispersed in silence.

It is impossible for anyone to have never encountered a crow or two. I don't know the number that has crossed your path, but match that number to this following ditty: "One is for bad news; Two is for mirth; Three is a wedding; Four is a birth; Five is for riches; Six is a thief; Seven is a journey; Eight is for grief; Nine is a secret; Ten is for sorrow; Eleven is for love; Twelve is for joy tomorrow."

Robert Burns, the Scottish poet writes, "My Mary's asleep by thy murmuring stream. Flow gently sweet Afton, disturb not her dream." I do not know if crows inhabit the banks of River Afton, but I can visualize the tempest of ire of this great poet, if cranky crows gather there.

2/5/10

No place for threats

Has there ever been such partisan rigidity or quarrelsome politics as we are seeing over the recent passage of healthcare reform? I cannot tell you how the fundamental direction of the Founding Fathers got altered. But I can tell you where it started. During the second term of George Washington's presidency. In James M. McPherson's historical publication, To the Best of my Ability – The American Presidents, he reviews how the assembled delegates would challenge Washington's assumptions, rather than follow his counsel, especially when negotiating treaties. This agitation led to his refusal to seek further election.

Speaker of the House, Nancy Pelosi is credited with marshalling the votes necessary for the passage of healthcare reform. But did you know in England, the Speaker of the House is not allowed to speak? How did this wisdom elude us? I presume choices that don't seek the truth stand empty. Yet history tells us, when you speak truth to power, it leads to martyrdom. Machiavelli said it better, "Public image matters, more than moral character." He claims it is easy to look cheating in the eye and not call it by its true name.

The New York Times revels in distorting the news to influence an election. Much of it is hollow and vacuous. In due proportion it is a kind of madness that foils the reason of debate (Obama calling Palin a pig with lipstick). Yet the passage of healthcare reform has precipitated a dangerous realm of unrestrained emotions. Threats of violence that is misguided and difficult to comprehend.

I can't wrap my mind around the cost (trillions) or the creation of a new bureaucracy to administer it. Can you visualize the endless committee meetings devoted to drafting this fiduciary black hole? It reminds me of that maxim: "A camel is a horse formed by a committee." Sometimes we get what we wish for. Just like sometimes we get what we vote for. We encountered a lot of pot holes with our past few presidents. Are you enjoying the ride with our latest? Or do you equate him with Benjamin Disraeli who said, "I grow intoxicated with my own eloquence."

4/2/10